All Shook Up

All Shook Up

Collected Poems about Elvis

Edited and with an Introduction by Will Clemens

Photographs by Jon Hughes

The University of Arkansas Press

Fayetteville 2001

05   04   03   02   01   5   4   3   2   1

Designer: John Coghlan

Library of Congress Cataloging-in-Publication Data

All shook up : collected poems about Elvis / edited and with an
introduction by Will Clemens ; photographs by Jon Hughes.
        p. cm.
Includes bibliographical references.
    ISBN 1-55728-704-X (pbk. : alk. paper)
    1. Presley, Elvis, 1935–1977—Poetry. 2. American poetry—20th
century. 3. Rock musicians—Poetry. 4. Singers—Poetry. I. Clemens,
Will, 1976–
    PS595.P72 A44 2001
        811'.54080351—dc21

                                                    2001000367

To my father (who prefers Brahms) and my mother (who prefers Mel Tormé)

Acknowledgments

"The Resurrection of Elvis Presley" from *Fate* by Ai; Houghton Mifflin Co., Boston, 1993. Copyright © 1991 by Ai. Reprinted by permission of the poet.

"Elegy for Elvis" from *A Closed Book: Poems* by Richard Blessing; University of Washington Press. Copyright © 1981 by Richard Blessing. Reprinted by permission of Marlene Blessing.

"All Shook Up" from *After the Splendid Display* by Don Bogen. Copyright © 1986 by Don Bogen. Reprinted by permission of the poet and of Wesleyan University Press.

"On the Elvis Mailing List" by Neal Bowers from *Zone 3* 2:1 (winter 1987): 21. Copyright © 1987 by Neal Bowers. Reprinted by permission of the poet.

"Conversions" by Neal Bowers from the *Sewanee Review* 101:3 (summer 1993): 310. Copyright © 1993 by Neal Bowers. Reprinted by permission of the poet.

"Mary's Dream," "Sphinx," "All the Stars Are Foxfire," and "I Stopped in Tupelo, Elvis," by Van K. Brock; *Bulletin for the Center for the Study of Southern Culture and Religion.* Copyright © by Van K. Brock. Reprinted by permission of the poet and with appreciation to the Center for the Study of Southern Culture and Religion and to a Rockefeller Foundation Grant for a Study of Elvis Presley.

"Elvis lives" from *The Last Night of the Earth Poems* by Charles Bukowski. Copyright © 1992 by Charles Bukowski. Reprinted with the permission of Black Sparrow Press.

"them and us" from *Book of Light* by Lucille Clifton. Copyright © 1993 by Lucille Clifton. Reprinted by permission of Copper Canyon Press.

"My Father's House" and "Elvis" from *Cross a Parted Sea* by Sam Cornish; Cambridge, MA: Zoland Books, 1996. Copyright © 1996 by Sam Cornish.

"Talismans" by Maudelle Driskell. Reprinted by permission of the poet.

With gratitude to the contributing poets, especially David Wojahn and Alice Fulton; to the University of Arkansas Press staff, in particular Beth Motherwell, Larry Malley, and Abigail Smith; and to my supportive friends and family, namely Faye Clemens, Jerome Clemens, Jon Hughes, and Herb Martin. Special thanks to David Nordloh at Indiana University for his help with several drafts of the introduction.

Contents

Introduction

September 1958: Army private Elvis Presley glumly boards a train near Fort Hood, Texas, bound for Germany.

At twenty-three years old, he has seen his 1954 4/4 version of Bill Monroe's waltz "Blue Moon of Kentucky" hit #1 on the Memphis c&w charts and his 1955 country version of Junior Parker's blues "Mystery Train" become his first #1 record. In 1956, Colonel Tom Parker and RCA purchased Elvis's contract from Sam Phillips and Sun Records for a then unheard of sum of $35,000, and Elvis's "Heartbreak Hotel"/"I Was the One" has rapidly become RCA's first million-dollar record. All his 1956 singles have been certified gold, with five #1 hits, "Heartbreak Hotel," "I Was the One," and "Hound Dog" among them.

At twenty-three, he has already played hundreds of gigs, from his days at the Eagle's Nest in Memphis (where Vernon and Gladys, Elvis's proud parents, would often attend), to the "Louisiana Hayride," the "Milton Berle Show," and the "Ed Sullivan Show." He has also made movies. His first feature-length film, *Love Me Tender*, produced for roughly one million dollars, has taken in that sum at the box office in its first three days. *Loving You, Jailhouse Rock,* and *King Creole* have followed. Between acting, concerts, and recording, he has practiced philanthropy: proceeds from a show scheduled by the New Frontier go toward lights for a youth baseball park, a public service announcement for the March of Dimes, his participation at the annual Road-E-O safe-driving contest for teenagers.

He has called a succession of places home: the two-room house in Tupelo, Mississippi, in which he was born; the low-income housing of Lauderdale Courts in Memphis; the new house on Audubon Drive in the suburbs. Then, in March of 1957, despite an impending draft notice, Elvis purchased a grand new home, Graceland. He paid $100,000 for this former church, away from downtown Memphis and in a grove of oaks,

which had been converted into a twenty-three-room southern colonial mansion. He spent an equal amount on interior design and renovation: a black bedroom suite trimmed in white leather, a white llama rug, a soda fountain with ice cream bar, mirrors on the ceilings. (The bizarre fake-fur-upholstered furniture and lampshades for the den would come later.)

For all its size and bought elegance, Graceland could not blot Elvis's fears about military induction. His mother shared that anxiety, compounded by a malaise brought on by the enormity of Graceland (where she and Vernon had their own plush room) and of the strange new world of fame and fortune. At the same time, both feared that his rise to fame had all been like a dream, that the magic would wear off during his army duty, or that he wouldn't be able to make a comeback after service. Though Elvis had been conscientious in sexual matters before, his desperateness in the week prior to his induction can be viewed in the fact that he was, in his own words, according to the biographer Peter Guralnick, "screwing everything in sight."

Soon after Elvis had arrived at Fort Hood for basic training, Gladys and Vernon moved temporarily to nearby Killeen. As the Texas months got hotter, Gladys became ill. On August 8, 1958, she and Vernon took a train back to Memphis, where she was admitted to the hospital with acute hepatitis. Two days later, Gladys's health took a turn for the worse, and Elvis, making some degree of progress in basic training, was informed of her grave condition. He took leave for Memphis to be with her. Though Gladys was certainly happy to see her son, she was very weak. The doctors could do nothing. Gladys died on August 14, a few days after Elvis's arrival in Memphis. Her death was extremely hard on him; years later, he would call it the great tragedy of his life. Despite the more than 100,000 sympathy cards he received, he cried and wailed. A kind of emotional breakdown followed: Elvis's temperature reached 102°—and apparently drugs were prescribed not just to bring his fever down but also to bring his spirits up. His leave was increased five days.

Boarding the train on that rainy day in September 1958, Elvis was physically—but not emotionally—recovered. Leaving fame, fortune, and success behind was one thing; coping with the unexpected death of his loving and supportive mother was another. And then poetry touched him.

A sympathetic GI in his company gave Elvis a copy of the enlarged 1956 edition of *Poems That Touch the Heart.* Compiled by broadcaster A. L. Alexander and first printed in 1941, *Poems That Touch the Heart* offered nearly four hundred pages of poetry, mixing major writers—Shakespeare, William Wordsworth, and Emily Dickinson—and minor ones. In his preface, reminiscent of the turbulence of world war and mindful of the impending unrest associated with the civil rights movement, Alexander outlines a hope that the collection will expose readers to the concepts of life that are elevating and invigorating, so much so that "our horizons begin to lift, our hardness of heart begins to soften, our gloom . . . lighten." Alexander's appeal and the emotional power of poetry that followed registered deeply with Elvis in his time of grief and loss. According to Guralnick, "one [poem] in particular really hit home": Albert Roswell's "Should You Go First," in four rhymed octaves. Guralnick says that Elvis "stared at it for some time, until he practically knew it by heart: 'I'll hear your voice, I'll see your smile / Though blindly I may grope / The memory of your helping hand / Will buoy me on hope . . .'" Is it too presumptuous to think that at that moment poetry helped Elvis put the pieces back together, pick himself up, and move on? In his recently published collection of essays and reviews, *The Poetry of Life and the Life of Poetry,* David Mason believes that poetry "helps people live their lives." Though the voice in a poem is specific to its author's life and feelings, it can, Mason believes, become one of our voices as well, "the imagination pressing back against the pressure of reality."

Indeed, Elvis did move on. A black and white photograph (copyright Leon Dishman, *Elvis: A Life in Pictures*) shows him en route to Europe aboard the U.S.S. *Randall;* newly promoted private first class, he is smiling while playing the accordion for two fellow servicemen. He would achieve the rank of specialist in June 1959, just months before he met his future wife, Priscilla Beaulieu (the daughter of a U.S. Air Force captain), in Bad Nauheim, West Germany. By the time of his honorable discharge in March 1960, he had been made sergeant. He returned to his career in music and movies, to finer performances, to worldwide adulation.

Fleda Brown Jackson in "Elvis Reads 'The Wild Swans at Coole'" imagines Elvis reciting William Butler Yeats's sonnet for the audience at the International Elvis Conference in Oxford, Mississippi. The captivated crowd listens "as if / they had got the secret of life into the poem." The obvious impossibility of Elvis reading Yeats aloud in celebration makes Jackson's poem humorous. Elvis was neither a poet nor a poetry enthusiast.

Though Elvis's relationship with gospel and pop song lyrics was deep, his acquaintance with traditional and modern poetry was thin. He had less use for it, for instance, than his father. Vernon gave Elvis and Elvis's still-born twin, Jesse, rhyming middle names: Aron and Garon, respectively, Aron "pronounced with a long *a* and the emphasis on the first syllable," as Guralnick has explained. And it was Vernon who insisted that a poem that he wrote be inscribed on Elvis's gravestone, which is next to Vernon's in the Meditation Garden at Graceland. The speaker in David Wojahn's "Pharaoh's Palace" terms Vernon's ordinary albeit heartfelt verse, "the clumsy epitaph his Daddy wrote." (The lines on Vernon's own gravestone are from Alfred Lord Tennyson's great elegy "In Memoriam.")

Elvis, the icon with only the thinnest acquaintance with poetry, is nonetheless the topic of much poetry. This anthology collects these poems and presents them in chronological order by date of original publication, beginning with Thom Gunn's "Elvis Presley" (1957). The topics are as varied as the poets.

Jackson's "Elvis Reads 'The Wild Swans at Coole,'" for instance, examines the debate over Elvis as creative artist versus imitative performer, real talent versus lite entertainer. Jackson depicts Elvis as "sick to death" with having to read Yeats's poem aloud. Similarly, Richard Blessing in "Elegy for Elvis" dissociates the image of the poet from the image of Elvis. The speaker in Blessing's poem contrasts the public reaction to Elvis's death with addressing the death of the U.S. confessional poet John Berryman. When Berryman died,

> not many women looked at their lives
> like closets of spikes and pointy toes
> and asked, *What good is any of it now?*

The obvious sense in these lines, that more women found meaning in Elvis's existence than they did in Berryman's, is made more subtle in the closing question. Blessing is also implying that Elvis has become so powerful as a rock star that his image overshadows the poet's more subtle work. Even a more popular poet than Berryman—Maya Angelou, say, or Allen Ginsberg—has gone largely uncelebrated in America. Blessing's lines serve to remind us that in our contemporary culture Elvis, who had become just as much a bloated mess as Berryman, will be more widely remembered.

When so many contemporary poets have written about Elvis, so few about any one poet, the question that needs asking is, "Why have these poets found Elvis such an intriguing subject to write about?" The answer often has something to do with the disproportion of his popularity or fame to a poet's. Ai's "The Resurrection of Elvis Presley," Neal Bowers's "Conversions," Maudelle Driskell's "Talismans," and Terry Stokes's "The Elvis Elevator" are arguably more concerned with investigating a different kind of disproportion. These poets tend to find the image of Elvis as a Christ figure, a persuasive popular impulse, absurd. Likewise, there is a hint of sarcasm in Van K. Brock's, Charles Bukowski's, or David Ray's considerations of a visit to Graceland as a religious pilgrimage. Yet if Elvis is not a divinity, he has an attractive appeal. Lynn McMahon's "An Elvis for the Ages" is among the poems that praise Elvis for his ability to rock with a confidence, an energy, and a style all his own. Elvis is admired for his ease in playing outside the boundaries of black or white or pop or country. He succeeded in "making-it-new." Similarly, Dan Sicoli's "All Shook Up" reminds us that the subversive, avant-garde-like innovators of punk rock have found inspiration in Elvis:

> in there these short hairs
> pumped up parodying
> the king
> swinging axes as if
> they once could hack
> at a melody
> screaming . . .

Then there are the poems that focus even more on the awesome physicality and sexuality of Elvis. In "us and them," Lucille Clifton pictures "elvis . . . still swiveling those negro / hips." Alice Fulton "reimages" Cupid as Elvis. And not just women have found Elvis a compelling body to write about. Dabney Stuart's "Fishing with Elvis," for example, takes what sometimes appears to be the inclusively male world of fishing and compounds this masculinity with Elvis, whom cultural theorists such as Eric Lott and David R. Shumway have discussed as the ideal male specimen in America. Stuart's poem goes one step further than this, though, and asks, somewhat moralistically, if there was anything as enlightening as fishing or poetry or music—something of a contemplative or reflective thinking substance— behind Elvis's awesome physicality? In other words, was there a Buddha behind the superman? By contrast, Elizabeth Ash Vélez's "Elvis P. and Emma B." challenges the idea of Elvis as a hyper-masculine monsieur when she compares him to Madame Bovary. These divergent views are indicative of the range of poetic statements in the anthology; they are a mixed bag, "All Shook Up."

The contributors' comments that follow the poems in this collection shed light on the authors' intentions. But as poet Pattiann Rogers says in her recent essay on writing as reciprocal creation, to try to accurately explain the reasons a poet writes a poem is to arrogantly assume an understanding that even the poet might not be able to fully articulate or demystify.

Different from the mass of fan poetry by Elvis fan club zines and the like (a canon which is typically laudatory and sentimental), the poems in *All Shook Up* represent, as a whole, a milieu of aesthetic and cultural concerns. Varied blank verse by Andrew Hudgins, loose sonnets by David Wojahn, and other forms are presented in these pages alongside the even more experimental free verse of postmodern poets Ai, Alice Fulton, and Diane Wakoski. Lucille Clifton, Sam Cornish, and Herbert Woodward Martin are among the black poets who have published poems about Elvis. *All Shook Up* collects poems not for their like formal, ethnic, or gender-specific qualities but for their shared subject matter, and what matter more interesting than Elvis, whose career and fame were so pervasive as to reach both the whole culture and individual lives?

In the end, Elvis may, in fact, be as much a product of poetry as cultural theorist Camille Paglia suggests. In her *Sexual Personae: Art and Decadence from Nefertiti to Emily Dickinson,* Paglia associates Elvis with George Gordon, Lord Byron, who wrote the expansive satiric poem *Don Juan:*

> Byron created the youth-cult that would sweep Elvis Presley to uncomfortable fame. In our affluent commercial culture, this man of beauty was able to ignore politics and build his empire elsewhere. A ritual function of contemporary popular culture: to parallel and purify government . . . Mass media act as a barrier protecting politics, which would otherwise be unbalanced by the entrance of men of epochal narcissistic glamour. Today's Byronic man of beauty is a Presley who dominates the imagination, not a [Duke of] Buckingham who disorders a state.

If Paglia is right about holding Byron and his creation of "the youth-cult" (as much in his life as in his poetry) responsible for Elvis's success, then we can begin to understand why so many poems have been written about Elvis. But Greil Marcus has been critical of Paglia's notion. In his book *Dead Elvis: A Chronicle of a Cultural Obsession,* Marcus implies that it involves not only a "brutal revision of the Western cultural canon" but also too much critical "riffing" in its "turning the body into body politic." With regard to Paglia's analysis of today's popular icon or image of Elvis, Marcus apparently finds more of a philosophical paradox. Riffing, too, it seems, he submits that the iconic image of Presley is in flux between meaning a passive, inanimate cultural object and the one man of beauty who actively disordered the American state. Perhaps Elvis *is* the "king of paradox," as Van K. Brock says in his poem "All the Stars Are Foxfire." The power of Elvis, a power which has given rise to so much fascinating poetry, may be elusive finally: we can't explain how he seems both larger than us and personal to us.

I believe an anthology of poems about Elvis invites readers to experience the connection between the historical and mythical status of Elvis, on the one hand, and the poetic imagery, on the other. I've tried to provide in this introduction a bit of the history and myth that is more thoroughly explored by Elvis biographers and cultural theorists. Jon Hughes's photographs offer visual enactments of the historical and mythical Elvis images that pervade our culture. Some of the photos were taken in Memphis, where these images are practically unavoidable. Yet others were shot in and around Hughes's hometown of Cincinnati, where the images are surprisingly abundant. Straddling the lines of art photography and photojournalism, Hughes's skillful black and white images complement the poets' words in ways that recall some of my favorite books of poetry: Anthony Hecht's *Flight Among the Tombs,* wood engravings by Leonard Baskin; Robert Hedin's *The Old Liberators,* artwork by Perry Ingli; and C. D. Wright's *The Lost Roads Project,* photographs by Deborah Luster.

Like Luster's photography in *The Lost Roads Project,* which documents Arkansas people and places not regularly imaged by mainstream media,

Hughes's photography typically emphasizes the human condition, though his work deals more with urban than rural culture. When Hughes and I were at Graceland, he was often more concerned with photographing the visitors and workers than the memorabilia. In this way, his art and documentary tend to undermine the commercialism that often attaches itself to the popular image of Elvis. Hughes's shot of the elevator operator, whom Stokes images in his poem set partly in downtown Cincinnati, is an example of his passion for artfully documenting the work and play of urban folk. In their introduction to *Elvis Rising: Stories on the King,* Kay Sloan and Constance Pierce have noted that "camp-fans might smirk" at the people who make up "an hallucination of community-in-Elvis." But Hughes does not smirk. His photo of the operator with her elevator shrine to Elvis offers his larger vision: Hughes suggests that the individual people and places he images are as important as Elvis.

Works Cited

Alexander, A. L. Preface. *Poems That Touch the Heart.* New Enlarged
  Edition. Ed. A. L. Alexander. New York: Doubleday, 1956.
  xix–xxii.

Frew, Tim. *Elvis: A Life in Pictures.* New York: Metro/Friedman, 1997.

Guralnick, Peter. *Last Train to Memphis: The Rise and Fall of Elvis Presley.*
  Boston: Little Brown, 1994.

———. *Careless Love: The Unmaking of Elvis Presley.* Boston: Little
  Brown, 1999.

Lott, Eric. "All the King's Men: Elvis Impersonators and White
  Working-Class Masculinity." *Race and the Subject of Masculinity.*
  Ed. Harry Stecopolous and Michael Ubel. Durham, NC: Duke
  University Press, 1997. 192–237.

Marcus, Greil. *Dead Elvis: A Chronicle of a Cultural Obsession.* New York:
  Doubleday, 1991.

Mason, David. *The Poetry of Life and the Life of Poetry: Essays and
  Reviews.* Ashland, OR: Story Line Press, 2000.

Paglia, Camille. *Sexual Personae: Art and Decadence from Nefertiti to
  Emily Dickinson.* New Haven, CT: Yale University Press, 1990.

Rogers, Pattiann. *The Dream of the Marsh Wren: Writing as Reciprocal
  Creation.* Minneapolis: Credo/Milkweed, 1999.

Shumway, David R. "Watching Elvis: The Male Rock Star as Object of
  the Gaze." *The Other Fifties: Interrogating Midcentury Icons.* Ed.
  Joel Foreman. Urbana: University of Illinois Press, 1997.

Sloan, Kay, and Constance Pierce, eds. *Elvis Rising: Stories on the King.*
  New York: Avon Books, 1993.

Thom Gunn

Elvis Presley

Two minutes long it pitches through some bar:
Unreeling from a corner box, the sigh
Of this one, in his gangling finery
And crawling sideburns, wielding a guitar.

The limitations where he found success
Are ground on which he, panting, stretches out
In turn, promiscuously, by every note.
Our idiosyncrasy and our likeness.

We keep ourselves in touch with a mere dime:
Distorting hackneyed words in hackneyed songs
He turns revolt into a style, prolongs
The impulse to a habit of the time.

Whether he poses or is real, no cat
Bothers to say: the pose held is a stance,
Which, generation of the very chance
It wars on, may be posture for combat.

1957

Herbert Woodward Martin

Miss Rosie Mae Watches Elvis Presley on "The Ed Sullivan Show"

Miss Rosie Mae,
sitting in her living room
watching "The Ed Sullivan Show,"
sucked in her pious lips,
smacked them clean as any sectarians',
watching from Los Angeles to the Adirondacks,
and uttered with her skeptical voice
of motherly concentration:
"Those little girls are too fast for words."
Every time his thigh would quiver,
as if he were writing
down some invisible numbers
or vast phrases to thrill the blood,
those tv girls would scream
a lightning jolt again and again.
Then Miss Rosie Mae would point to the screen
as if a million girls had, all of a sudden,
given up the privacy of their bodies wholly,
especially when Sullivan announced:
"For the first time on our stage,
here to perform for you this evening,
is the new singing sensation Elvis Presley."
The cheers never allowed us to hear again.
I never knew a guitar had so many seductive moves;
I never knew a guitar could win so many innocent lips.

They testified loudly when his guitar twitched;
they shivered, as if touched by the Holy Ghost,
when the chords tickled the loneliness
in their thighs.
"It is dangerous to watch that young man
from the waist down. He's pure sex,"
Miss Rosie Mae said.
"Somebody, somewhere needs to give those
little girls a pinch of saltpeter,
maybe a little more than a pinch if you ask me."
Elvis uttered his songs on a ledger of air;
he sang with such a vengeance
that every young girl felt
as if he were singing only to her,
that she had received her proper potion

and could cheer, unreservedly,
her blood into infinite hoarseness.

1958

Van K. Brock

All the Stars Are Foxfire

Staying up to eat and play all night
to your inner burning,
you could turn off or turn on,
almost anything you wanted,
as you slept through our day.
Given the seedy space spread before you,
a dotted slate, rare times you were alone,
whatever you read was transformed by
your own thoughts, as our half-worlds
turned dark to light, and your poverty
became the emptiness of wealth.
No one is sound when body and the earth
are both in ill health, and any lie
the truth, no matter how well all seems.
We know the freezing leaf is also burning.
Elvis, here in the night, maybe you are free,
having risen from dirt to live forever,
perhaps, even though all I could see in you,
trying to raise myself from the same dust,
was a Hollywood country singer who knew no more
than the words of songs written by others.
Sadly, true, Little Brother, but you gave all
to your songs, to become the king of paradox,
your fans looking up at you with raw desire,
as at a bonfire they could come no nearer to.
You knew nothing of time, only eternity,

for the poor learn to look away from time,
and the faraway stars still wink at me,
as they winked at your empty nights
of great hunger pulsing to be opened
to itself, for the sieve to be filled.
Wizard of wishes, you drove your new Phaeton
into the office of the egg and offered
your services to the Prince of Shadows
against the sinister substances of dream,
but whoever he was, you are dream itself,
and I stand with those holding up
your wrought iron gates. The fire
in your voice can steady the stars
no more than their longing, as they hold on
to the forged cold of a shape twisting
in beaten metal, their fierce longings
also like those bright points in the sky
as they stand in August nights watching blasts
frozen a million years still puncturing
darkness with their shimmering holes.

1979

Van K. Brock

I Stopped in Tupelo, Elvis,

to see the house you were born in.
Like a swollen boxcar, a door
on each end, you once said would fit
in your living room at Graceland.
They'd fixed it up—fresh paint,
new screens, but I still see gray wood
through opaque paint, gnats and flies
going in and out unguarded windows.

Two steps across the porch,
where you used to sit clattering
on your cheap guitar, your dead twin
always beside you, and three steps
inside the door, I stop in the middle
of the room. A woman in a slow-rocking
prop almost fills the space,
not very big in her new-fashioned
granny dress. She barely looked up
as I took three steps more
to the kitchen, with the small heater
Gladys cooked on and knew how close
it was in winter, how wretched in summer.
And of course your high chair. That's it.
The place out back where the outhouse stood
has a concession stand with restrooms.

And it is all choreographed: people
all over the yard look lost
(more filled-out girls than normal,
but all sizes and ages). All sexes, all
types, if some more than others.
The woman with her hair dyed black,
like yours, in a too-tight black western
pantsuit, chic for a woman of thirty,
who still looks good at forty,
and her son, about sixteen,
also looking like you, judging
by the crowd, that's easy, but I couldn't
tell whether it was you, himself,
or her he was mourning for.

Elvis. People linger, nothing to do,
waiting for you to come out and invite
them in to stay a while. And you would,
well-mannered child that you were—
if you were here—like it had been a mansion.
All they wanted. And back, next to my car,
a serious reporter still asking
a well-dressed couple in their thirties:
"What did he mean to you? Why are you here?"

1979

Van K. Brock

Mary's Dream

I was living in New York.
He was dancing on the skyline.
I dreamed he was playing his guitar.
I couldn't believe he was dead.
He was made of iron welded to the stars
but danced in the air like flames.
The city blurred. It was part of him
waving at me. Then it was me.
That's when I knew he would never die.
He would always be the king. Look!
I'm too heavy and not pretty, but we
were one. One hand on my neck
squeezed tight, gently, as he held me,
his separate fingers moving all over
my body like musical notes on the sheet.
I was a cloud filled with colored lights,
but as lightning, when it strikes,
moves everywhere, everywhere it touched
sprouted flames. I was the music.
My whole body. It came from his mouth
and out of me, every pore, every wisp
of angelhair shivering and singing,
and it was then he called me by my name.
"Mary, I want you to go to Graceland.
It'll mean a lot to me."
So I came.

1979

Van K. Brock

Sphinx

I am driving west in the afternoon,
Tallahassee to Tupelo—then Memphis,
through Montgomery, Birmingham,
all that sordid history—
to see why the papers and tube
are all converging on Elvis
with people all over the world,
on his first death day.
The sun is at my back,
because you are there.

I'm inquiring after miracles
in the city of the Phoenix and Sphinx,
to observe what rises where garbage
is still the provender of the poor
and Kings still die for our dreams,
and ten miles west of you,
where a Beetle was crushed by a truck
in monsoon rain, lights flash around
a poncho, another bodybag.
How fragile bodies seem.
And according to the rules for drivers,
I risk my life to write this
as I drive alone in my car,
watching the road through rain.

You are not even a goddess,
although alive in your absence,
and even if you were dead,
I would still talk to you,
not caring what people would say,
should they study me.

1979

Richard Blessing

Elegy for Elvis

August 1977

Elvis lay cool in his thick shadow
and saw it was an island no one
would come to ever again. It was Memphis
and summer. It was winter. Snow was falling
blue as Christmas. It was so still
he heard his heart fill like a lonesome hotel.

Listen, John Berryman used to like to say,
Whyncha ask me whattis like to be famous?
What did he know, King? What did he know?
He never sold a million. When he died
not many women looked at their lives
like closets of spikes and pointy toes
and asked, *What good is any of it now?*

Dr. Nichopoulous was saying, *Come on, Presley,*
breathe for me, but you were happy. You'd played
your last request. Snow settled around you
like a thousand paternity suits. Ice
filled the island trees. You had gone farther
than a gossip magazine. You planned to name
your shadow for the first American to say,
I never heard of him.

Presley, you always breathed for me,
rock-bellied, up from Tupelo, a place
pastoral enough for elegy. Now one of us
is dead. Tender as Whitman's lilac sprig,
I leave these plastic flowers in the snow.
What perishes is only really real.
I twist the dial and you are everywhere.

                                    1981

Thom Gunn

Painkillers

The King of rock 'n' roll
grown pudgy, almost matronly,
Fatty in gold lamé,
mad King encircled
by a court of guards, suffering
delusions about assassination,
obsessed by guns, fearing
rivalry and revolt

popping his skin
with massive hits of painkiller

dying at forty-two.

What was the pain?
Pain had been the colours
of the bad boy with the sneer.

The story of pain, of separation,
was the divine comedy
he had translated
from black into white.

For white children too
the act of naming the pain
unsheathed
a keen joy at the heart of it.

Here they are still!
the disobedient
who keep a culture alive
by subverting it, turning
for example a subway
into a garden of graffiti.

But the puffy King
lived on, his painkillers
neutralizing, neutralizing,
until he became
ludicrous in performance.

The enthroned cannot revolt.
What was the pain
he needed to kill
if not the ultimate pain

of feeling no pain?

1982

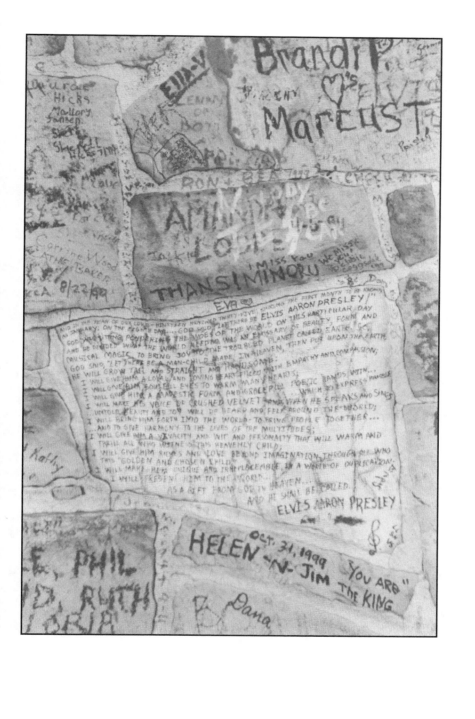

Don Bogen

All Shook Up

Elvis couldn't twitch a hip
or Ed would get the sack,
so they bundled his dream thighs
in flabby charcoal slacks

and tried to keep the cameras high
while Ed paced in the wings,
glaring at the monitors
where Elvis snarled, beading

sweat on a curled lip. Four
aging sharkskin crooners hummed
chords to muffle the beat,
blurred in swing harmony like some

USO group, sweet
as Karo. The fat microphone
was too far off to grab,
the slung guitar he'd brought from home

was cut off at the strap, the drab
curtain just waited to drop.
So did Ed. His really big show
was floating at the top

of Eisenhower Sundays. Who could know
the tiny screens would pop,
the cloth-smothered speakers split with the news
that we were all shook up?

1986

Neal Bowers

On the Elvis Mailing List

It started with the Greatest Hits album,
ordered one night in a haze
of nostalgia and wine, toll-free
in the middle of *Notorious,* just after
Claude Raines started poisoning Ingrid Bergman.

In a room at the top of a long
flight of stairs she was weakening,
thinking all the while how much she
wanted, needed, and loved Cary Grant,
who was taking too long to understand
it was now or never.

By the time he rescued her,
our album was being processed
somewhere in New Jersey, and we were
already in line for motorcoach
tours to Graceland, porcelain busts,
and an opportunity to give, tax-free,
to the Presley Trauma Center.

Everything worked out well,
except for Claude Raines, of course,
who was taken inside behind a heavy door
by two men who would laugh at anyone
wailing "Don't be cruel."

1987

Joyce Carol Oates

Waiting on Elvis, 1956

This place up in Charlotte called Chuck's where I
used to waitress and who came in one night
but Elvis and some of his friends before his concert
at the Arena, I was twenty-six married but still
waiting tables and we got to joking around like you
do, and he was fingering the lace edge of my slip
where it showed below my hemline and I hadn't even
seen it and I slapped at him a little saying, You
sure are the one aren't you feeling my face burn but
he was the kind of boy even meanness turned sweet in
his mouth.

Smiled at me and said, Yeah honey I guess I sure am.

1987

David Rivard

Cures

The part of the soul that doubts, again and again,
is scratchy as this song, "Mystery Train," where Elvis
relates some dark to himself. Even the light
in the living room seems sullen. We've turned the stereo
up loud, don't have to talk. After the latest argument,
trading blame is all that is left. After all that,
forgiveness? More punishment? Forgetting?
You curl, knees up, on the couch. Along your bare neck
the skin looks soft—shadows, the barrage
of falling brown hair, soft. I'm in the raggedy armchair,
and the music just washes through those questions,
then pours out the screen door. So this is what we do,
how we feel, each doubt a little larger
than desire, so that nothing
seems enough. And for a while,
ten minutes, I've stared at the album cover.
The face with the half-sneered, boyishly charming smile
stares back from the floor. The words echo wall to wall,
then silence as one song ends and we wait for the next.
What do we think? His smoothness and raveling wail will cure us
of all this? These rockabilly blues
from the early Memphis days, a shy country kid
opening for Pee Wee Crayton at the Flamingo Club.
When all he cared about was shouting the next tune.

The next tune. But endings are truer
for all their need: a mansion outside town,
years of Seconal, gaudy stage suits. Ways to simplify
the hundred confusions screaming in the body,
to become a star, or something stranger. . . .
I'd like to go over and brush away the hair
from your face. All the questions,
all the night, as it strikes
the house like a train whistle. And after I get up,
cross the room, you and I aren't sorry
it leads to this kiss. Or to what it brings on,
a soothing that lasts only so long,
like stardom
in America, or now this silence between songs.

                                              1988

Dan Sicoli

"All Shook Up"

in there these short hairs
pumped up parodying
the king
swinging axes as if
they once could hack
at a melody
screaming
"i'm on drugs. . . . i'm all
fucked up!"
and below these
dressupforeachothermommy suburbanites
slam dance to it all at center stage

spiked pinned dyed ripped
pseudo-neo-punks pretend life is a war
in packs they worship
little gods
suicide is still an alien virgin

if you're serious
become the night
lick dry heels of fallen winoes
abandon weapons
let wounds bleed freely
shave head with dull razor
eat public trash

sleep in cracked concrete cunt womb soul darkness
vomit at every opportunity

spit on doctor preacher police politician
train eyes to be frozen dead cat
french kiss anus of city
wake with it on your breath
call yourself nigger one
and exhale

and when you begin
to lust the ultimate
start counting backwards
from 10. . . .

1988

James Seay

Audubon Drive, Memphis

There's a black and white photo of Elvis
and his father Vernon in their first swimming pool.
Elvis is about twenty-one and "Heartbreak Hotel"
has just sold a million.
When he bought the house,
mainly for his mother Gladys they say,
it didn't have a pool,
so this is new.
The water is up to the legs of Vernon's trunks
and rising slowly as he stands there
at attention almost.
Elvis is sitting or kneeling on the bottom,
water nearly to his shoulders,
his face as blank and white
as the five feet of empty poolside at his back.
The two of them are looking at the other side
of the pool and waiting for it to fill.
In the book somewhere
it says the water pump is broken.
The garden hose a cousin found is not in the frame,
but that's where the water is coming from.
In the background over Vernon's head you can see
about three stalks of corn
against white pickets in a small garden
I guess Gladys planted.
You could press and point and say that in the corn

and the fence, the invisible country
cousin and mother, the looks on Elvis and Vernon's
faces, the partly filled pool, we can read
their lives together, the land
they came from, the homage they first thought
they owed the wealth beginning to accumulate,
the corny songs and films,
and that would be close but not quite central.
Closer than that is the lack
of anything waiting in the pool we'd be
prompted to call legend
if we didn't know otherwise.
They're simply son and father wondering if it's true
they don't have to drive a truck
tomorrow for a living.
But that's not it either.
What it reduces to is the fact that most of us
know more or less everything
that is happening to them
as though it were a critical text
embracing even us and our half mawkish
geographies of two or three word obituaries:
in the case of Kennedy, for example, I was walking
across a quad in Oxford,
Mississippi; King's death too caught me in motion,
drifting through dogwood in the Shenandoah.
As for Elvis,
there were some of us parked outside a gas station
just over the bridge from Pawley's Island
with the radio on.
That's enough.
I know the differences.

But don't think they're outright.
The photo is 1034 Audubon Drive, Memphis,
and then it's Hollywood,
still waiting for the pool to fill.

1990

Dabney Stuart

Fishing with Elvis

We've been out for an hour
and caught nothing much,
talking about lures and the lie
of the water, the way the lures
lie in the water. Finally
I tell him I have friends
who like his music.
Are any of them black?
I want them to forgive me.
I tell him to forgive himself.
His luckless bloat threatens
to capsize the canoe. I have
to remind him to keep still.
The absence of a stage
must feel like a lost limb—
his hip twitches now and then.
He casts into the weeds
and hooks a small bluegill, pulls
it out of the water in an arch
over us. It splats down
and he skids it across the surface.
What do I do now? he asks.
Whatever you want, I say.
It's your show. He opens the bail
and lets the fish swim away;
when his line gives out

he cuts it. *Story of your life?*
I ask. He looks at the empty
reel, the nourishing water.
It's never too late, I mumble;
it probably always was, but what
good would it do to say so?
Instead, I take a chance, tell him
I wish you hadn't played
the sweet roles so much,
been so obliging, believed you were
what they kept asking you to be.
Didn't you ever want to
take up with a K-Mart clerk
at the bowling leagues?
His rod tip trails in the current.
His eyes burn from the thick paste
they're buried in. *Where were you*
all my life? he wants to know.
Listening, I tell him.
Was there something else you wanted?

1990

David Wojahn

W.C.W. Watching Presley's Second Appearance on "The Ed Sullivan Show": Mercy Hospital, Newark, 1956

The tube,

    like the sonnet,

        is a fascist form.

I read they refused

    to show this kid's

        wriggling bum.

"The pure products

    of America. . . ."

        etc.

From Mississippi!

    Tupelo,

        a name like a flower

you wouldn't want

    beside you

        in a room

like this,

    where the smells hold you

        a goddamn

hostage to yourself,

    where talk's

        no longer cheap.

Missed connections,

    missed connections—

        a junk heap

blazing there in
        Ironbound,
                a couple kids
beside it,
        juiced on the
               cheapest wine. Mid-
thought. Midwinter,
          and stalled
               between the TV screen
and window. . . .
        This pomped-up kid,
              who preens
and tells us
      "Don't Be Cruel."
           Kid, forget it.
You don't know
      a fucking thing
          about cruelty yet.
              1990

David Wojahn

The Assassination of Robert Goulet as Performed by Elvis Presley: Memphis, 1968

—"That jerk's got no heart."—E.P.

He dies vicariously on "Carol Burnett,"
Exploding to glass and tubes while singing "Camelot."

Arms outstretched, he dies Las Vegas-ed in a tux,
As the King, frenzied in his Graceland den, untucks

His .38 and pumps a bullet in the set.
(There are *three* on his wall, placed side by side.)

The room goes dark with the shot, but he gets the Boys
To change the fuses. By candlelight he toys

With his pearl-handled beauty. Lights back on,
But Goulet's vanished, replaced by downtown Saigon:

Satellite footage, the Tet offensive,
Bodies strewn along Ky's palace fences.

Above a boy whose head he's calmly blown apart,
An ARVN colonel smokes a cigarette.

                                        1990

David Wojahn

Nixon Names Elvis Honorary Federal Narcotics Agent at Oval Office Ceremony, 1973

The King is thinking Tricia's got nice tits,
Of Grace Slick at Tricia's wedding, trying to spike
The punch with acid (orange sunshine, 300 hits),
While the bubblegum Turtles churned out their schlock,
And the Ehrlichmans danced the Funky Chicken.
Grace Slick named her baby *God,* a moniker,
He thinks, almost as good as *Elvis Aaron*—
Who's today shaking hands with the Chief, his mind a blur
Of dexies and reds, but scored with an M.D.'s prescription.
Pompadour, karate *ghee,* and cape,
Twenty pounds of rhinestones, a corset to tuck the paunch in:
Late model Elvis. His hands shake as he takes the plaque.
Explaining the hieroglyphic on his ring, he laughs.
"It means, sir, *Taking Care of Business with a Flash.*"

                                                    1990

David Wojahn

Elvis Moving a Small Cloud: The Desert Near Las Vegas, 1976

—after the painting by Susan Baker

"Stop this motherfucking Limo," says the King,
And the Caddie, halting, raises fins of dust
Into a landscape made of creosote,
Lizards, dismembered tires. The King's been reading

Again—*Mind Over Matter: Yogic Texts*
On Spiritual Renewal by Doctor Krishna
Majunukta, A Guide on How to Tap the
Boundless Mental Powers of the Ancients.

Bodyguards and hangers-on pile out.
His Highness, shades off, scans the east horizon.
"Boys, today I'm gonna show you somethin'
You can tell your grandchildren about."

He aims a finger at Nevada's only cloud.
"Lo! Behold! Now watch that fucker *move!*"

1990

David Wojahn

At Graceland with a Six Year Old, 1985

It's any kid's most exquisite fantasy,
To have his name
                              emblazoned on a private jet.

So Josh stares through the cockpit of
                              The Lisa Marie,
Its wings cemented to the Graceland parking lot.

The kitsch?
                    All lost on him, the gold records and cars,
Dazzling as the grave's eternal flame.

And I read him the epitaph's Gothic characters.
"A gift from God . . ." etc. Daddy Presley's wretched poem.

Colonel Parker was asked, after Elvis's death,
What he'd do now to occupy his time:
                              "Ah guess

Ah'll jus' keep awn managin' him." He's really *Dutch.*
The accent, like the colonel tag, is a ruse,

Like the living room's wall of mirrors—rigged immensity,
Pipsqueak Versailles,
                              where Josh makes faces, grinning at me.
                                        1990

David Wojahn

Pharaoh's Palace

(Memphis, 1988)

Last week a half-crazed Mormon woman in a blue-white
    bouffant claimed
miraculous healing at the grave, hurling away her crutches
    to walk
a few unsteady feet, until a gang of courteous
    uniformed

guards restored her to her braces,
    and dispatched
her in a golf cart to the entrance. She wept in ecstasy
    or sorrow
as the iron sixteenth notes of the gate
    clattered shut.

Labor Day weekend: the day's final tour. Above us,
    the shuttered
room where the overdose took place, although
    the guards claim
heart attack. Around us in the living room,
    row upon row

of phony potted daisies, his favorite flower,
    and we walk
the arena of the dining room, its behemoth TV, the ceiling
    still patched

where the chandelier, a ton of crystal
    in the form

of a guitar, crashed last year to the table,
    a formal
setting for sixteen. In the basement snack bar
    we shudder
at the color scheme, the three TV sets side by side.
    Our guide, an incongruous patch

on her eye, tells us he "watched three stations *at once!*"
    Mirrors climb
walls and ceiling, TVs in infinite recession. Mirrors
    line the walkway
to his "Jungle Den," waterfalls cascading from
    imitation stones. The Pharaoh,

he claimed, of rock and roll. The gift shop girl
    looks up from a row
of souvenir glasses and posters. In his late-phase
    karate uniform,
rhinestones and white leather, he poses sulking
    wherever we walk.

I think of how his crooked Greek physician shot him up,
    the shut-in,
pacing his bedroom, rolling up his silk kimono
    sleeves, exclaiming
like a child when the methedrine surged in, and how
    he once dispatched

his private jet from Memphis to Las Vegas—the gleaming
    Beechcraft *Apache*—

to ferry back peanut butter and jelly sandwiches
      from some skid row
deli he remembered. But he was a *nice boy,* always,
      and claimed

his needs were simple: nymphets in white panties,
      the snow that formed
on each TV screen after "The Star-Spangled Banner" played,
      and the stations shut off
and he'd stare awhile at nothing. We weave
      down the sidewalk

to the grave, the clumsy epitaph his Daddy wrote.
      A woman walks off
sobbing to herself. Her husband in cowboy boots,
      face a patch
of oily sores, follows her shaking his fist, slaps her twice
      and tells her *Goddamn you, shut up.*

He drags her off by the arm, but still she's
      wailing, sorrowfully
crouched on a bench. On the parking lot loudspeaker
      he's performing
"Young and Beautiful." On the two-lane headed home, we stop
      at a house claimed

by kudzu and grass, barn and house collapsed, wood a uniform
      gray, windows shuttered.
Evening comes on: we walk a path to a family plot,
      a hornet's nest patching
a single marker proclaiming no name, only HERE US
      O LORD IN R SORROW.

                                                1990

Ai

The Resurrection of Elvis Presley

Once upon a time, I practiced moves in a mirror—
half spastic, half Nijinsky,
with a dash of belly dancer
to make the little girls burn.
I dyed my dark blond hair black
and coated it with Royal Crown pomade,
that stuff the Negroes used,
till it shone
with a porcelainlike glaze.
Some nights I'd wake in a sweat.
I'd have to take off my p.j.'s.
I'd imagine I was Tony Curtis
and I'd get a hard-on,
then, ashamed, get up
and stare at myself in the mirror by nightlight
and, shaking as if I had a fever,
step, cross step, pump my belly,
grind my hips, and jump back
and fling one arm above my head,
the other toward the floor,
fingers spread wide
to indicate true feeling.
But where was he
when I bit the hook
and got reeled in
and at the bitter end of the rod
found not God but Papa Hemingway,

banished too to this island
in the stream of unconsciousness,
to await the Apocalypse of Revelations
or just another big fish?

2

I don't know how it happened,
but I became all appetite.
I took another pill, another woman,
or built another room
to store the gifts I got from fans
till neither preachers, priests,
nor Yogananda's autobiography
could help me.
The Colonel tied a string around my neck
and led me anywhere he wanted.
I was his teddy bear
and yours and yours and yours.
But did I whine, did I complain about it?
Like a greased pig,
I slid through everybody's hands
till I got caught between the undertaker's sheets.
And now I wait
to be raised up like some *Titanic*
from the Rock 'n' Roll Atlantic.
Now as I cast my line,
tongues of flame
lick the air above my head,
announcing some Pentecost,
or transcendental storm,
but Papa tells me it's only death who's coming

and he's just a mutated brother
who skims the dark floor
of all our troubled waters
and rises now and then to eat the bait.
But once he wrestled me
like Jacob's angel
and I let him win
because he promised resurrection
in some sweeter by-and-by,
and when he comes to me again
I'll pin him down
until he claims me
from the walleye of this hurricane
and takes me
I don't care how,
as long as he just takes me.
But Papa says forget him
and catch what I can,
even if it's just sweet time,
because it's better than nothing,
better even than waiting
in the heavenly deep-freeze,
then he tells me don't move,
don't talk,
and for Chrissakes don't sing,
and I do what he wants,
me, the king of noise,
but in my memories
this country boy *is* singing,
he's dancing in the dark
and always will.

1991

Cornelius Eady

Young Elvis

He's driving a truck, and we know
What he knows: His sweat
And hips move the wrong product.
In Memphis, behind a thick
Pane of glass, a stranger daydreams

Of a voice as tough as a Negro's,
But not a Negro's. A voice that
Slaps instead of *twangs,*
But not a Negro's. When it
Struts through the door
(Like he knows it will), and
Opens up, rides

The spiky strings of
The guitar, pushes
The bass line below the belt,
Reveals the drums
As cheap pimps,
In fact transforms the whole proceedings
Into a cat house, a lost night . . .

He wets his lips,
Already the young driver is imagining
A 20th century birthday present,

The one-shot lark of his recorded voice,
The awe he intends to
Shine through his mother's favorite hymns.

1991

Andrew Hudgins

Versification of a Passage from *Penthouse*

So he'd be sure to see me, we came in late.
He likes tall girls with black hair so I wore
a real tight mini-skirt. We made eye contact.
Finally he put the mike aside, walked over,
stretched out his hands. I stood up and he hugged me.
Then we French-kissed. We French-kissed a long time,
at least for thirty seconds—making out
while all the people at the Stardust watched,
and Greg, my husband, too. I thought I'd faint.
But Elvis wouldn't let me go. And Greg—
Greg was the best sport in the world, you know.
But, really, how could anyone get pissed
about my kissing *Elvis.* And while he sang,
he kept up heavy eye contact with me
and once he sort of stumbled in a song,
just like, you know, the kiss had shook him up.

Up in his suite, he strummed a red guitar
and sang to me. I thought I'd melt. My clothes
just sort of flew off me. We didn't fuck.
Mostly I sucked his cock and licked his balls.
He loved it. And I love to do it too—
suck cocks, I mean. After an hour or so,
someone knocked on the door. Elvis knelt down,
kissed me goodbye, and left to do his show.
I told Greg I'd gone out to get some air.

He really got ticked off and slapped my face.
"In Vegas, you went out to get some air?"
he yelled. It does sound pretty stupid now,
but what do I care. I sucked Elvis Presley's cock.

1992

Neal Bowers

Conversions

Before he died
he never came anywhere near here
but now turns up
in back seats at the drive-thru
or wearing a bad disguise
at the all-night pumps.
Death has freed him
to go everywhere, all at once,
looking like a bad imitation
of himself, sounding familiar but odd
on a dozen call-in radio shows
where he is taking questions
in that purgatory between midnight
and the face in the mirror,
the neck of a bottle against
the rim of a glass a dead bell
in the background.
He says some day he will
explain everything,
and then the line goes monotone,
"or is that his mantra?"
asks the wiseguy D.J., breaking in
for a string of commercials—
weight loss, wrinkle cream, hair restorer—
the lost, the faithful,
buying it all at 3 A.M.,
saying, "This is the body."

1993

Lucille Clifton

them and us

something in their psyche insists on elvis
slouching into markets, his great collar
high around his great head, his sideburns
extravagant, elvis, still swiveling those
negro hips. something needs to know

that even death, the most faithful manager
can be persuaded to give way
before real talent, that it is possible
to triumph forever on a timeless stage
surrounded by lovers giving the kid a hand.

we have so many gone. history
has taught us much about fame and its
inevitable tomorrow. we ride the subways
home from the picture show, sure about
death and elvis, but watching for marvin gaye.

1993

Sam Cornish

My Father's House

when my father
whipped me
with his strap
like a master
his humble
slave
beat me
with his fist
like his woman
when she was out
of line
he found God
as my blood filled
my shoes   when he
brought me crying
and bleeding
to Jesus   he saw Elvis
sweetly
singing
with his hips

1993

Sam Cornish

Elvis

his thing   is singing
like a black
smoked   down rhythm
and blues   white
boy the preacher
trembles   "that boy
is the devil   sounding
like a laughing crazy jiving
nigger"

1993

Brian Gilmore

Elvis

1.

elvis presley is alive and well
and the world scrapes near the ground

at the north pole, a flag remains unplanted
in egypt, there are no pyramids.

elvis presley is alive and well
but there is no such thing as superman,
>*there was never a thing called slavery*
>*there was never a rape of africa.*

elvis presley can beat jesse owens
because jesse never ran a race
>*bob gibson is throwing knuckleballs*
>*kareem is shooting jumpers.*

elvis presley is alive and well and i swear i
saw him in harlem
>everyone bolt your doors!
>everyone board up your windows!!
>everyone stop taking singing lessons!!!
>no one is writing this down!!!!

elvis presley was a black man

and al jolson didn't need any make up,
         for it is proven
         and i believe it to be true

         elvis taught bruce lee karate!

2.

elvis shouldn't have been allowed
to
register
and vote

3.

shoot him with fire hoses

4.

such a mass,
such a disturbing mass. such a wallowing in the mud
mass   such a dangerous mass.

couldn't live up to it,
couldn't be it, ain't that great,
ain't that bad, ain't that cool.

the mass didn't make up those moves, didn't make up
that voice, those clothes, those ways of crooning

and swaying and fooling the world with that whole
weird way of doing things.

they brought it. swallowed it. bathed in it.
ate it   with a gin and tonic but shit,
hold the tonic because i don't understand it,
i can't face it unless my head is spinning!

the mass couldn't do it all because mud is like
blood;   mud is about emotional outrage!

the mass could never be it all because
america is an illusion and for those of us
watching
tv
all the time—iranians don't care about some white
boy acting like a nigger snorting velcro.

that goes the same for the middle east
and asia
and afghanistan
and afrika
and most of the
world.

but now you're saying—"japan loves elvis,
seen those impersonators . . ."

but japan ain't been japan since 1945;
japan is manhattan or chicago or london

damn sure ain't japan!

you're saying the same about other
countries too who are into it
long after we were into it

but really they aren't into it
because once you are into it
you can't call yourself an
afrikan or
an asian
or an arabian.
call yourself whatever you want,
but don't upset the ancestors,
they know about the mud and that
emotional outrage.

still there is that mass.

that huge monster looming over us larger than life
a wailing soul simulating bantu and yoruba wearing
zoot suits and breaking more black sisters' hearts
than chuck berry could mend with "maybelline" or
"thirty days."

so the mass swelled and got muddy. the mass got so
big and muddy it couldn't see or walk, realized it
couldn't be superman
couldn't be the lone ranger
couldn't be captain america throwing his mighty
shield.

the mass knew different.
knew about chitlins, whiskey

and juke joints.
knew he stuck out like a sore thumb.
knew he didn't make it because he was better than
anyone
else
because memphis had 500 young white boys around
1950 whose old man or grandmother bought them a
guitar and some ray charles' records for christmas.

he just knew better than the rest that velcro was a
magic potion.
and magic makes people snort velcro.
and snorting velcro makes people wallow in the mud at
night.

and mud makes us look like something we aren't.
because
the mass wasn't white,
he had too much mud in his hair
and snorted too much velcro.

and the mass wasn't black because
he had too much velcro in his hair
and not enough mud hanging off his lips.

the mass was just dangling on a vine holding a
guitar
and some watermelon wondering

why did he want to be what he truly despised?

5.

sick the dogs on him!!

6.

where the hell is bull connor?

7.

elvis lovvvvvvvvvvveeeeesssss
pig knuckles.

1993

Fleda Brown Jackson

Elvis at the End of History

It was him, Elvis, sheepishly
stepping out of my outhouse,
looking better than ever, the way
some old men slim down and loosen
their lines. He had left the door open,
the lid slightly ajar on the women's
hole. As usual, I forgave him
everything. I acted normal, as if
I hadn't been waiting under the trees,
last night's full chamber-pot
balanced in my hand. I could have
said at any point in my life
that he was the one I was waiting for,
looking sleepily down from the stage,
seeing but not seeing me,
granting me reprieve in an instant
from my life, but holding me in it
like a star. It's like if you ask
for Jesus, Jesus comes. It's never
the way you think. There he was,
hair flopped over his eyes,
coming out of the last outhouse left
along the lake, and it there
only because of the grandfather clause.
This was the end of our history
together, all that strangeness

in the crotch, the pulse hammering
the bass line, real life and art
straining to fuse, to end all
history. I was hearing in my mind
Won't you wear my ring,
around your neck? but it sounded
like the sweet core of good taste,
like the gospel fleshed out,
saddened down to honky tonk.
"Excuse me," he said. "The older I get,
the more often I have to pee."
I agreed. I might have been humming
to myself, sometimes I don't know
when I'm doing it. I can be
treble and bass at the same time.

                                    1993

Lynne McMahon

An Elvis for the Ages

What the billboard
proclaims in this careful composition where black
    diamonds find a rhyme in the motley
the model wears, and the pink grass he's outlined
against repeats in clouds caught on
    reflector shades,
        is a slogan we can put our hearts in—

a future atavism
that lifts us up by the snarl, by the brilliantined
    forelock, and sets us down
in the back seat. When he cants his hip
    in homage,
in memory, in making-it-new, when he starts
    that slow gorgeousness
and his shoulders begin their train over

the trestle tremor,
the I-can't-stand-it vibrato, dropped to one knee,
    sweatdrop stoppered in a phial, phylactery,
when he hits the high long drawn overnote,
stretched over hushed drums, eternity pulls itself
    across the black gap
of the universe, thinned to a wire and holding

seconds past the breaking
point until it does finally thank god break,
    the blood

drains away and he's gone, that's it, nothing: no
heart, no breath, the earth shocked still for
    the eon
it takes the guitar to kick in and he's at the mike
    resurrected, the butterfly
in the leather pulse damaged, but unmistakable.

1993

Elizabeth Ash Vélez

Elvis P. and Emma B.

Bear with me:
Memphis is not far
from Yonville-L'Abbaye,
and would you have guessed
at the cornfields, blond,
set against a tidy French sky
and a wilder Tennessee one?

Elvis and Emma
went in for spending
were Philistines
were suckers
for gilt and glitz
were wracked and ruined
by Romance.

Monsieur Lheureux and
Colonel Parker
were fat and happy.

We knew from the beginning
that the Hotel-de-Boulogne,
as well as any Hilton,
was full of heartbreak.

                                        1993

Diane Wakoski

Blue Suede Shoes

The blond whose skin was translucent as a glass slipper,
        whose small-boned frame allowed silk to drape
        as if underwater crenellating fans of sea anemone
        were breathing when she walked,
wore a sapphire blue maternity dress
and sat in the living room of The Home for Unwed
        Mothers
playing cards with her less-glamorous enciente friends.

I on the sofa, reading Shakespeare's love sonnets, or was it
TESS OF THE D'URBERVILLES? 1956. Pasadena, California.
Most of us there are teenagers.
Though she's the beauty;
I'm the book-worm brain. And I heard her say,
    that blond, the girl who'd been to a party with a
    college fraternity boy and wound up here,
    as ashamed as all the rest of us
        the nurse who found out she was going to have
        the hydrocephalic baby,
        the fourteen year old raped by her father,
        and lots of girls like me whose boyfriends loved us
        (we thought),
        but were not ready to be fathers,
she who wore a diamond on one of her sea cucumber
pale fingers and always had a cool
remark on her witty red tongue, said

"This baby will probably be born with blue
        suede shoes."
I imagined her blond baby boy,
    a princeling, with royal
        Cupid lips and his mother's
            nose, straight as a golden pin;
                he'd be a blue blood,
            I thought. A "king" in baby shoes.
My literary ear recognized a title, though I knew little else,
listening to Beethoven or Chopin as I did,
not even the Beach Boys, now such a classic sound to me,
    representing the Orange County of my youth,
        of beach parties, and parked cars, and
            high school class rings.
I hadn't heard of Carl Perkins who wrote the song before Elvis
recorded it, though I knew
    where Memphis was; hadn't heard of
        Sun Studios, or "The King"/
the Sun King, I thought; Incas, blood sacrifices, virgins
having their hearts cut out over jungle pyramids.
    I knew that royalty was in my blood,
my swollen belly, and I knew that my love,
    like that love alluded to in the sonnet,
was the kind
that was so great
I'd "scorn to trade it" for a kingdom.

I felt the martyrdom of adolescence, but savored the
irony,
that I was the brain,
she, the woman with
    the delicate princess face

who fantasized that her
      taboo baby might be born with little blue
      suede Elvis-shoes on his little
blond feet, was the beauty,
and Chance had us both sitting here in the same parlor,
glass slippers shattered,
    bare foot and pregnant,
No, no, no,
that wasn't us!

There *were* shoes. If not for us
    Cinderella's crystal slipper. Or Dorothy,
    innocent Dorothy, drug addict Dorothy's ruby
    slippers of Oz,
        then there were

for our sons,
those swinging blue suede shoes;
and we would be left with music,
music in our heads, both of us,
she listening to Elvis
and I to the dissonant sounds of late Beethoven.
She with her skin translucent as a glass slipper
and I with my shy-girl skin, blushing, blushed ruby-slipper red,
both of us dancing, bare footed, just dancing,
in our ruby slippers or glass slippers or blue suede shoes,
dancing hard to survive our shame.

1993

Alice Fulton

About Face

Because life's too short to blush,
I keep my blood tucked in.
I won't be mortified
by what I drive or the flaccid
vivacity of my last dinner party.
I take my cue from statues posing only
in their shoulder pads of snow: all January
you can see them working on their granite tans.

That I woke at an ungainly hour,
stripped of the merchandise that clothed me,
distilled to pure suchness,
means not enough to anyone for me
to confess. I do not suffer
from the excess of taste
that spells embarrassment:
mothers who find their kids unseemly
in their condom earrings,
girls cringing to think
they could be frumpish as their mothers.
Though the late nonerotic Elvis
in his studded gut of jumpsuit
made everybody squeamish, I admit.
Rule one: the King must not elicit pity.

Was the audience afraid of being tainted
—this might rub off on me—
or were they—surrendering—
what a femme word—feeling
solicitous—glimpsing their fragility
in his reversible purples
and unwholesome goldish chains?

At least embarrassment is not an imitation.
It's intimacy for beginners,
the orgasm no one cares to fake.
I almost admire it. I almost wrote despise.

                                        1995

Alice Fulton

Some Cool

Animals are the latest decorating craze.
> *This little piggie went to market.*
> *This little piggie stayed home.*
It's a matter of taste.

I have this string of pig lights for the tree.
Each hog is rendered into darlingness,
rendered in the nerve-dense rose
of lips, tongue, palm, sole. Of the inside
of the eyes and nose.
> They wear green bows.

Driving home these bitterly Michigan nights,
I often pass the silver bins of pigs
en route to the packing house. Four tiers to a trailer.
A massive physical wish to live
blasts out the slits
as the intimate winter streams in.
A dumb mammal groan pours out and December pours in
freezing the vestments of their skin
to the metal sides, riddling me
with bleakness as I see it. As I see it,

it's culturally incorrect to think
of this when stringing pig lights on the tree.
It's chronic me.

Our neighbor, who once upon a life
hauled pigs to slaughter,
said they are confined in little iron cribs
from farrowing to finishing.
Said steel yourself
this might be unpoetical and spoke
about electric prods and hooks
pushed into every hole.
About: they cried so much he wore earplugs.

While trimming the tree, I stop to give thanks
for the gifts we've received,
beginning with *Elvis's Favorite Recipes,*
I'd like to try the red-eye gravy—
bacon drippings simmered with black coffee . . .

"Some had heart attacks. Some suffocated
from others stacked on top.
They were pressed in so tight—
hey, what kind of poetry you write? Well.
They suffered rectal prolapse, you could say."

Why not spend Christmas with Elvis?
Invite your friends
to bring their special memories of the King.
Put a country ham in the oven and some of his songs—
White Christmas to Blue—

About: somehow a pig got loose. A sow
fuzzed with white like a soybean's husk.
It was August and she found some cool
under the truck. When he gave her a Fig Newton

her nose was delicacy itself,
    ticklish as a lettuce pushed whole into his hand.

Are You Hungry Tonight?
I speak from the country of abundance
curdled brightly in the dark,
where my ethics are squishy as anyone's, I bet.
I'd like to buy the enchanted eggnog fantasies.
Instead I'm rigging the tree with grim epiphanies
and thinking myself sad.

        For a gut level of comfort,
        close your eyes, smell the pork chops frying,
        put on "Big Boss Man" and imagine
        the King will be coming any minute.

"At the packing house, some bucked like ponies
when they saw the sun. Some fainted
and lay there grunting to breathe.
Drivers hooked the downers to the winch
and tried to pull them through a squeeze.
Their legs and shoulders tore right off.
You'd see them lying around.
After the showers, they turned a hysterical
raw rose. They shone. The place seemed lit
by two natural lights, coming from the sky and hogs.

Pigs are so emotional. They look at the man
who'll stun them, the man
who'll hang them upside down in chains.
They smell extinction and try to climb
the chute's sides as it moves.

At the top, the captive bolt guy
puts electrodes on their heads
and sends a current through.
I've heard the shock could paralyze
but leave them conscious, hanging
by their hocks from the conveyor
until their throats are slit.
Pigs have an exquisite will to live."

After eight months he quit
and got a job screwing tops on bottles
of Absorbine, Jr.

Now when people ask what kind of poetry I write
I say the poetry of cultural incorrectness—
out of step and—does that help?

I use my head
voice and my chest voice.
I forget voice
and think syntax, trying to add
so many tones to words that words
become a world all by themselves.
I forget syntax
and put some street in it. I write

for the born-again infidels
whose skepticism begins at the soles
of the feet and climbs the body,
nerve by nerve. Sometimes I quote
"At mealtime, come thou hither,
and eat of the bread,

and dip thy morsel in the vinegar."
Sometimes I compose a moaning section,
if only for the pigs.
Like surgeons entering the thoracic cavity—right,
the heart's hot den—
I've heard we could slip
our hands into the sun's corona
and never feel a thing.

1995

Alice Fulton

From "Wonder Stings Me More Than The Bee"

—Emily Dickinson, Letter #248

1. Elvis from the Waist Up

Are you self of my self
or shudder—
alien—other—

the body wants to know.
As for this promiscuous spring
wind, it should be neutered.

I say it should be
fixed—rich as it is
with the invisible invasive

sex lives of the trees.
As for me, I was wheezing
from one faux colonial château

to another on The Showcase of Homes
having laid down my five dollars
to let them try to sell me

a neobaronial heartbreaker
inlaid with wet bar charm. Let me guess
which room's the largest.

No contest. It's the cars'.
The sprightly realtor spots me
for a fellow

connoisseur: "It is evident
the minute you enter
that the interior is

unlike any you've seen."
I want to say "These are the places
that give imitation a bad name."

But knowing what it is
to stand in knotted throat and control
top, with schmoozey syndrome

grins and shakes to sell
the unendurable
durable goods, I say

"No kidding." I praise
the medieval turret *avec* deck.
"It's not fake anything. It's real

Dynel." What did that slogan sell?
Then I cast off
the hospital-issue snoods

they make you wear
over your soles to save
their finished wood.

My body doesn't miss a beat.
It's marshaling its forces
against the goodly grasses.

Mistaking benign outsiders
for low-life viruses. Accusing
the weeds of treason.

I'm sneezing as if I agreed,
though drugs have boned a granite corset
under my relaxed-fit breathing

knits. The immune system's so adept at this
telling self from other stuff
it would reject

a skin graft from a sister, brother.
Heart of my heart,
you go too far, I think as I bless

the inventor of Kleenex.
Who had the greater genius,
the one with the idea

or the one who made us
say the brand name
as we reach? A slowcoach

from the pills, next thing I know
I'm off the map and thirsty
for some liquid summer—

a Sex on the Beach or Fuzzy Navel—
in the inflated meadows
of The Country Club.

My Diet Coke's already poured
when the girl says "I'm sorry.
We only sell to members.

People with accounts."
I'm too put out
to even ask for water.

And returning to my Legend,
a bee flies up and stings me
near my wedding ring.

". . . dummies
that engineer a metallic sheen
or add a little glass

are more attractive than actual
females," the orchid show flashed back.
Something about—the bluff,

the Elvis-from-the-waist-up.
"Do you wear falsies?"
a wasted uncle asked

our junior bridesmaid—shaved and teased
to nubile grace—her gown
like egg whites beaten

to a nuptial lace.

1995

Alice Fulton

From "Give: A Sequence Reimagining Daphne & Apollo"

Mail

What they had in common went beyond the I'm cool-are-you-
cool handshakes and passion
for bloodsport. From forever, they were too alike to get along.
She was incidental
at first, a bit player in their boy-god drama—which began
when each of them
claimed "My Way" as his song. Both were superheroes
in the action-
figure category. Both were fond of cherry bombs. But their
biggest
similarity was this: deep down they were profoundly
superficial.
This kinship prevented them from seeing anything
but difference
in each other's style. Phoebus Apollo favored snapbrim hats,

alligator shoes and sharkskin
suits from Sy Devore's Hollywood men's store. In battle,
stripped to the mail
he wore beneath and crowned with light, he glowed like a
refinery
turning crude into product, roaring Doric columns of flame. "I
make everything

and make it into everything else," he liked to claim. He took pride
in how cultured he was, a musician of pansexual magnitude
with his suave
ballads of desire. His friends—who had to listen to him

brag
about the last rival he'd skewered against the high F
cymbal,
the broad he'd slammed against a two-way mirror—called him
Your Eminence
to his face and The Monster privately. Of course, he had
his own line
of designer products. His PR people washed the death out of
his image
and got him onto cookies and air fresheners, among other
things.
He could lip-sync in ten languages and was globally marketed
as General Voice
Swoon Pope and Chairman of the Bored, though provincial

to the bone,
he called any place outside Parnassus "Darke County,
Ohio."
Jove was "the Big J"; a good time "a little hey-hey."
Himself he dubbed
The Republic Thunderbolt; Cupid, The Bell Airacobra
Venus Flytrap
and Fluttering Pharmacy of Love—which seems unfair since
Phoebus
gained his own fame as a healer by prescribing Chivas
Regal.

Cupid's skin was napped with floral fuzz and exhibited
a creamish structure,
like mayonnaise but more dense. He resembled a flesh-eating
botanical.
Yet that gosh-darn boyish charm of his made it hard
to credit
the two-shot derringer glued to his thigh. He'd aim
at chandeliers
and light switches, fire into his Ferrari if the battery went
dead.
But his bullets always ricocheted, striking someone
in the heart.
He sleepwalked and needed looking after.
Phoebus
considered him a frivolous child, carney spirit, gyrating
primitive
and part of nature, which only amused the little god.
"I fly
because I take myself so lightly," he'd smile. You'd hear

a helicopter drone.
Then this vision appeared, frosted with glittering filaments
from the soles
of his feet to his little mauve wings—whose nectar-secreting
glands
kept him fat and sticky. Or else it was the fried peanut
butter and banana
sandwiches he always craved. Apollo ate nothing
but pasta
with a dab of porpoise sauce. He despised Cupid for dressing
in a blouse
slashed to the waist and a tiny gold-lined cape from Nudie's

Rodeo Tailors.
For the mixed metaphor of his jumpsuit that flared to wedding
bells white
as a pitcher plant's. Apollo was still exulting over

his recent easy
listening hit when he happened on Cupid's opening
at the Vegas Hilton.
"What right hast thou to sing 'My Way,' thou imbecilic Fanny
Farmer midge larva,
thou sewer-water-spitting gargoyle, rednecked bladderwort,
dirtbag, greasedome
and alleged immortal of a boy," Apollo fumed. "Do thou be
content
to smite the teen queens with thy rancid aphrodisiac and cover
not
my swinging tunes. 'My Way' is my song; with it I have
penetrated
the pestilential coils of rock and roll that smothered
the charts
with plague-engendering form, for which I received
the Presidential
Medal of Freedom and a Ph.D. To think I did all that, and
not like Thor,
and not like Zorro. Oh no. I did much more—" And Cupid
interrupted, "Your way

is all head and no heart. I'll get you cock-cold, you technical
reptile.
I'll neuter you, dude. I'll delete-obscene-verb your brains
till they bleed.
When the King's feeling vengeful, this old world sees stars.

He holds
his crossbow like a Fender guitar. He makes
a hybrid
from a dog and a god. Their hearts go WOOF when he shoots
his wad."
So saying he twitched his wings and flew directly to
The Aladdin Hotel in Vegas.

There he pressed two records of opposite effect: one fostered
an autonomy unravished
as the winter wind's; one, an imperial grunt, made the listener
wish
to dominate and call it love. The first, unlabeled, went to
Daphne,
who adored the wilderness between territory and names.
The other,
on the SUN label, was mailed off to Apollo who mistook it
for a tribute
from his star cult and was pierced. Cupid hadn't forgotten
how Apollo
thee-and-thoued him. He gave the God of Truth new words.
"Well, strike me pink,
what a fix I'm in," Phoebus found himself saying.
"I'm belching
like the hound that got into the gin. Pard' me for trying to
give trees a hug.
I'm in love. Umm! I might throw up." Daphne,
meanwhile,
began stockpiling weapons, studying strategic arms in friendly
competition

with Apollo's sister Phoebe. Like Phoebus, Phoebe loved
a fast bird,
a good gun and same-sex parties. Each member of her all-girl
band
had a signature whistle the others used as summons.
Daphne
swirled with them through the forest, neither mortal nor
immortal,
but a creature inbetween. Her beauty was mutable.
Take
her hair, redly restless as a vixen's or dolphin-
silver
from minute to minute. Frothing like white water it was
channeled
by a single ribbon so tributaries escaped and trickled down her
face. A dangerous
draw followed in her wake. Downstream, her current seemed
friendly, ready
to negotiate and give. Upstream you had to fight the deep
meanders of her
mind. Many wanted her and how to coax a river daughter

from her chosen
bed became the question. She would not
be dammed.
Hissing, camouflaged by a palladium haze, she'd bounce
sound
off distant objects to predict their motion, shape, and place.
Echolocation
is what she used to navigate, traveling up to one hundred miles
a day.
Her sonar let her see right through opacities: read

the entrails
coiled inside the trees. The skeletons of beasts looked
lightning-struck
to her: locked in the moment when the bones glow
through
the skin, and given three outwardly kind people, she could
find the one
whose heart was sour. But her gift for visualizing the inner

chambers
of words was most impressive. She'd tell of *wedlock's* wall
that was a shroud
of pink, its wall that was a picket fence, the one of chainlink
and one
that was all strings. While Apollo hardened with love for her,
Daphne
stripped the euphemism from the pith. *Love* was nothing
but a suite
of polished steel: mirrors breeding mirrors in successions
of forever, his
name amplified through sons of sons and coats of arms,
her limbs
spidering, her mind changed to moss and symbol, a trousseau
of fumed wood,
the scent of perforations as his relief rose above her
smokey field.

                                                    1995

Alice Fulton

A New Release

(Daphne)

A voice changed to a vinyl disc, a black larynx,
spun
on the hi-fi as we called it, before light was used to
amplify
and the laser's little wand got rid of hiss. The
diamond-tipped
stylus stroked the spiral groove and guitars flared out of
reticence:
the first bars of a hit. I always wanted to hear it
again,
though it was always in my head: sticky,
invasive,
and what else in that culture was that
dark?

Easing the new release from its sleeve, I saw myself
bent
out of shape in its reflections: a night whirlpool or a
geisha's
sleek chignon, an obsidian never reached by skin
since skin
always has a warmth of blood beneath. It was a synthetic
Goodyear black,
like all records, pressed with a tread the needle traced,
threading

sound through ear and nerves and marrow. I touched its
subtle
grain sometimes wondering how music lurked in negative
space
that looked so unassuming. The marvel was—the missing
had volition.
And the spaces between tracks were a still profounder
black: darker than bitter-
sweet Nestlés, coffee ground from chicory, or Coke. Black
as it must be inside

a tree. "Wear My Ring Around Your Neck," the latest
hoodlum Cupid sang.
He aimed at objects and hit people, it was rumored.
His urgent nonsense—
about hound dogs, rabbits, class and lies—changed
aren't to *ain't,*
were to *was, anything* to *nothing.* "Caught" was the operative
verb.
While couples jived and twisted I must have listened
differently—
as to a special pressing—with my head
against
the set. Somehow, by the last chill tingle of the cymbal
I wanted
to be the singer rather than the wearer of the ring.
To this day,
rodents gnawing at the wooden walls remind me of the rasp

of dust
before a cut. A cut. That's what we called a song.
And handsaws—

harvesting the forest in the distance where I live—
sound
like the end: the rhythmic scribble of stylus against
label
when everybody's left. Everybody's gone
to bed.
And the record turns and turns into
the night.

1995

Charles Bukowski

Elvis lives

the boy was going to take the bus out
to see the
Graceland Mansion

then
the Greyhound Lines went
on strike.

there were only two clerks
and two lines
at the station
and the lines were
50 to 65 people
long.

after two hours in line
one of the clerks told the
boy
that his bus
would leave
as soon as the substitute
driver arrived.

"when will that be?" the
boy asked.

"we can't
be certain," the
clerk answered.

the boy slept on the floor
that night
but by 9 A.M.
the next morning
the substitute driver
still had not
arrived.

the boy had to wait
in another line
to get to the
toilet.

he finally got a
stall, carefully
fitted the
sanitary toilet seat
paper cover,
pulled down his
pants,
his shorts
and
sat down.

luckily
the boy had a
pencil.

he found a clean
space
among all the
smeared and demented
scrawlings and
drawings

and very
carefully
and
heavily
he printed:

HEARTBREAK HOTEL

then he dropped the
first
one.

1996

Fleda Brown Jackson

Elvis Sings Gospel

The picture of Elvis late at night at the piano,
singing gospel. Everyone has left. There are a few
folding chairs and the upright piano. Elvis
is lifting almost out of his black-and-white shoes;
there's no music to look at. It's so simple, the way
loneliness sits down in the middle of a bare room
and the middle gives way, and here you are, in the real
music that meant itself to be played. He is leaning
to the keys, bringing them to whatever the point was—
the typical point of getting washed in the blood of the Lamb,
or building a sure foundation, or going home
to the Lord—but he is hearing the words as exactly themselves,
individual, no reference to anything. I am not
imagining this. I know it: the way the words
save you by themselves, the hush of the word's entrance
like a spirit-lamp. Nobody wants anything
more than they want *home*—what *home* means—
struck like a gong against itself, reverberating
Gladys, maybe, or Uncle Vester, the Assembly of God
Church, Mississippi Slim, Big Mama Thornton,
Ernest Tubb, all the way out to the barely audible
crowds, the great weariness to come. But inside
is the word, encouraged slightly into music, taking
the shape of the room until neither one exists
any more, doesn't have to, since it is home already.

1997

Fleda Brown Jackson

Elvis Goes to the Army

"Goodby, you long black sonofabitch," he says
to his limo as he climbs on the bus to basic training.
The U.S. Army has him on the scales, then,
in his underpants, baby-fat showing, mouth downturned
in sorrow or fear. Not that we should make him out
a martyr, but he could be losing his career, here,
and he could have gotten out of this. It *is*
worth noting, when a person leaves his mama
and his singing behind and gives over to the faint signals
picked up by his inner ear. So what if the signal
in a particular case is mundane: the unremarkable
desire for love, for lack of ambiguity.
He's more alert than he's ever been, time clicking
away with the greater ritual's small appointments:
dressing and undressing, tightening bedcovers, reciting
the valuable gun, becoming part of the diorama
where danger is everywhere, a good reason to blend
khaki with the earth. Now, thirty years later, uniforms
are back in favor, following the lead of the Catholic
children in navy and white, soldiers of God
and high-scorers on SATs alike, sure
of their place in the universe. "This is the Army, son":
even a King like Elvis might hear that
and relax at last between what's come before
and what will be: the dead hair of the past
buzzed off in a second, the skull of the future

rising under a battalion of stubs that hope
to live up to the example of the fallen. We will not laugh
at the shorn head, but will consider a long time
the incomprehensibility of our desires, and the way
we beg ritual to take them off our hands.

1997

Fleda Brown Jackson

Elvis Acts as His Own Pallbearer

Life up to now had been no mistake,
getting out of East Tupelo,
out of the sharecropper's shack.
Fame was nice.
But this is America,
where you keep redeeming yourself
by leaving the past behind.

It wasn't him in the coffin; anyone could tell
it was a wax dummy. The hair was coming loose,
nose too pug.

How many times had he disappeared
like a magician?
He used to get the body shaking,
the left leg wiggling,
then half-sneer, turn away
from the audience as if he were kidding,

as if he were shaking them off.
We saw how it was done.
You had to make up the moves every day
of your life, start over so many times
you were obvious,

completely American, almost invisible,
so you could leave again,

carry yourself out to the garden
and see what came up next.

1997

Fleda Brown Jackson

Elvis Reads "The Wild Swans at Coole"

During the First International Elvis Conference in Oxford,
Mississippi, Elvis, alive as ever, is asked to read aloud
"The Wild Swans at Coole," to see what a Hunk

-a Hunk-a Burnin' Love could do to expose the other,
more subtle, longings to the average citizen who might
be raised to contemplate a little, for God's sake,

instead of falling into a blind beat, producing unwanted
babies and maudlin tears! Elvis fingers the page,
tries to plan what to do, sick to death without the music's

jingo, the strings that drive it, and the lyrics that fasten
to the music and ride on through, so the body can be
the words. Meanwhile, they wait for their poem.

He starts at the first, trees in their autumn beauty,
nine-and-fifty swans that take off, or don't, so what?
Among the rows of wan faces, nothing for the thoughts

to take off on, nothing to ease the thoughts. Poem
clamoring on instead of a song, words that aren't supposed
to be said Southern, lines that end before you're finished

thinking, and the last question breaking through the levee
at the end of the lines. He thinks what to do, then, with
his naked and weightless body. They are listening as if

they had got the secret of life into the poem, now,
even with him flying off the end of it, trying to swagger,
one hand in his pocket, bravely cocking an eyebrow,

off into the wilds where the girls are screaming, wanting
his babies, no questions asked, ah yes, the subtle grass
of the wilds, and the drum-beat of the human heart.

1999

Fleda Brown Jackson

The Women Who Love Elvis All Their Lives

She reads, of course, what he's doing, shaking Nixon's hand,
dating this starlet or that, while he is faithful to her
like a stone in her belly, like the actual love child,
its bills and diapers measured against his blinding brightness.
Once he had kissed her and time stood still, at least
some point seems to remain back there as a place
to return to, to wait for. What is she waiting for?
He will not marry her, nor will he stop very often.
Desirée will grow up to say her father is dead.
Desirée will imagine him standing on a timeless street,
hungry for his child. She will wait for him, not in the original,
but in a gesture copied to whatever lover she takes.
He will fracture and change to landscape, to the Pope, maybe,
or President Kennedy, or to a pain that darkens her eyes.
"Once," she will say, as if she remembers, and the memory
will stick like a fishbone. She knows how easily she will comply
when a man puts his hand on the back of her neck and gently
steers her. She knows how long she will wait for rescue,
how the world will go on expanding outside. She will see
her mother's photo of Elvis shaking hands with Nixon,
the terrifying conjunction. A whole war with Asia will begin
slowly, in her lifetime, out of such irreconcilable urges.
The Pill will become available to the general public, starting up
a new waiting in that other depth. The egg will have to keep
believing in its timeless moment of completion without any

proof except in the longing of its own body. Maris will break
Babe Ruth's record while Orbison will have his first major hit
with "Only the Lonely," trying his best to sound like Elvis.

1999

Fleda Brown Jackson

The Death of Gladys Presley

The doctor put her on a "soft diet," then,
which she interpreted as Pepsi-Cola and watermelon,
but that didn't kill her, her liver did, some clotting
problem, and after it was over, the wild excesses
of grief you might have guessed: "Look at them hands,
Oh God, those hands toiled to raise me," bringing
in the Bible word *toiled* for added weight.
The kind of grief it's hard to believe in,
from the outside, it seems to delight so in the show.
"Elvis, look at them chickens. Mama ain't
never gonna feed them chickens no more,"
Vernon said, picking out objects to reverence
for their recent lostness. It's the truth, though,
the way Elvis touched things, then, with handfuls of fire,
and the way the wind hit his face as the celestial
door opened and the voice that had been in secret
between mother and son shone tremendously,
at that moment, before death finished penetrating
her body, feet last. "Look at her little sooties,
she's so precious," Elvis cried, leaning over the coffin
and hugging and kissing her feet, then her hands and face
until they had to cover her in glass, the one
pure object waiting to be raised. "Everything I have
is gone," he cried, and this was the truth, poor child
made of practically all suffering, having to come back

to it over and over to get it right, to suffer
all the way through the outer skin to get down
to the earliest thing you call human, to rest there alone.

1999

Fleda Brown Jackson

I Visit the Twenty-four Hour Coin-op Church of Elvis

—Portland, Oregon

Well, sure, it's only
a window in a brick wall,
and eight small, seven large, circular framed Elvis-faces
that spin when you put fifty cents in.
The computer screen asks you what you want: wedding, confession, or
what.
I got my personal Elvis I.D. card:
The bearer of this card is a SAINT in the Church of Elvis.
He or she may also be Elvis. Please treat them
accordingly. Thank you.
The faces were spinning like 45s,
and I was combing my hair in the plastic reflections,
fixing my lipstick. It was a subtle change.
I think I am probably Elvis. I have begun to feel like
a lost child in Portland, anyway,
to feel uncertainty about my life,
to feel a religious determination to make my words sing.
I was crossing Rockville Road to meet you here for lunch,
keeping my hips loose, my sunglasses on.
Didn't I order a cheeseburger for the first time in years?
And I feel I am gradually being purified
of my irony,
back to the true rock and roll.
I want to run my fingers through what hair you have left

and call you Baby, throatily,
and mean for you to Treat Me Accordingly.
We could do our wedding vows again.
I feel we could get all the way back to the original vows,
before our separate cosmic fractures,
the vows we made years ago to other people
that had no irony whatsoever,
that were all Love Me Tender, all Heartbreak Hotel.

1999

David Ray

Sunday Morning

A pile of discards on the sidewalk,
so I stoop to ponder
what they've discarded—

found unworthy of their further
attention. *The Holy Bible,*
of course, on top of the heap,

stolen from some hotel or motel
room, as it says it was placed
by the Gideons, a few clothes

that look perfectly wearable—
trousers, not bad neckties,
one that may have belonged

to my father, a black bow clipon,
two pairs of shoes, one blue suede—
unconvincing evidence

that Elvis still lives. A pair
of glasses—I pity the poor bastard
who lost them, recall the day

I backtracked over half of Provence,
circled the rocky road twice,
rewarded only by smell of rosemary

and thyme and distant view
of the sea, island where poor
Valjean served his time and escaped.

I open the Bible—my old habit
of taking a dip. Dante did it
with Vergil, sure that one image

could lead him out of hell.
And seldom has it failed me.
I stand amazed above the pile

of castoffs—a silken blouse,
a bowtie, a blue shoe. King
Solomon speaks of burnt offerings.

1999

David Ray

The Brides of Elvis

She holds a candle, advances
toward the shrine, not an altar
or statue of Our Lady of Lourdes,
but the gravestone of Elvis.

She has told another, "We're like
nuns. They're married to Jesus,
and we're married to Elvis—
I don't mind if it's polygamy."

"Me too," says the other, "I love
them both," and they compare
gold rings, inscribed as if
from the living lover, the husband.

"Did you ever notice how much
the names sound alike, Jesus
and Elvis? I'm glad they're
in heaven together." Both brides

of Elvis have tattooed bodies,
no part neglected. "Sometimes
in the night I can feel him," one says.
"Me too," the other snaps back,

"I'm having his baby, want
to feel?" But envy is aroused,
and they no longer speak
as they advance, candles

aglow with the spirit of Elvis.

1999

Maudelle Driskell

Talismans

At the flea market across from the Commerce Speedway
you can buy Elvis relics in zip-lock bags
with masking tape labels—the napkin smeared with peanut butter
and banana grease, the pocket comb with a single strand
of black hair twined in its teeth, rhinestones
dandruffed from the white Las Vegas jumpsuit. All point
with the insignificance of dogs that have already treed the coon
toward the masterpiece—Elvis's wart.

Showcased under the glass of an overturned jelly jar,
impaled on a bright-yellow balled stickpin stuck in a cork,
the wart, looking for all the world like an albino raisin,
seems to hover, bound only by that ball end.

"That's the last vestige of The King. Only $500.
You know, each cell has everything you need
to make a whole person. You could clone Elvis from that wart."
A crowd gathers in awe, imagining
the billion tiny possibilities risen before their eyes.

Something simple happens—devotions, beliefs,
strong through some accident of conductivity—
too much salt, too little salt, in the cell spaces of the neuroconductors,
some brief spell of ball lightning rolling through our brains—
quickening an interest in the local auto mechanic,
sending us on crusades, giving us the idea for Velcro,

telling us to kill our wives, leading us forward
in blind faith, making us hear The Word
and hope that, unlike steak, we move on to Glory,
seeing, for the first time, the glistening strings of dew
in moonlight, strung all along the spider's tender lines,
leaving us shaken in the divine smell of strawberries.

1999

Terry Stokes

The Elvis Elevator

Even here in Cincinnati,
where it's against the law
to get excited, there are
Elvis shrines. The latest
condemned to an old downtown office building.
You walk into the elevator,
which is covered in a dark shroud; photos
of Elvis & his beloved mother, Gladys,
the one who gets three times the print
than the old man, Vernon,
on the headstones
right next to the pool in the shape of a guitar,
right there in Memphis, just outside the house
where Elvis took his last crap, & just across
the way, the Elvis shopping mall
where I played the Elvis pinball machine
& hit for two bucks,
which wasn't enough to buy recycled flowers
from Elvis's grave
or the book with the blue people in it
that the Krishnas were hawking.
O.K., so I'm looking around this elevator:
Elvis & Ann Margaret,
Elvis & Priscilla,
Elvis & Natalie Wood,
who would later

get flushed out of the world
in her own way,
& his thirty-three movies
equals Christ's life,
& the green gospel records,
& then the eight-foot man steps into the elevator,
"They belong to the woman who normally runs
this thing." & I drift back:
all eight members of my eighth-grade class
of Colebrook Consolidated School
joined the Elvis fan club,
before the Colonel had the smarts
to squeeze every penny he could out of a
teenager's pocket—for free.

Oh yeah, the Elvis elevator takes you
to the eighth floor,
the camera repair joint,
where they tell you in eight seconds,
"This thing can't be fixed;
there's a camera store on the first floor."
And the eight-foot-tall man sings,
"Oh, Sole Mio," at the top
of his lungs.

2000

Contributors' Notes and Comments

Ai is the author of six books, *Vice* (W. W. Norton, 1999), *Greed* (W. W. Norton, 1993), *Fate* (Houghton Mifflin, 1991), *Sin* (Houghton Mifflin, 1986), *Killing Floor* (Houghton Mifflin, 1979), and *Cruelty* (Houghton Mifflin, 1973). She has won many prizes and awards, including a Guggenheim Fellowship, two NEAs, and the 1979 Lamont Prize. *Sin* was nominated for a Pulitzer Prize. Ai has published her poems and stories in many magazines, including *American Poetry Review,* the *Iowa Review,* and the *Los Angeles Times Book Review.* She has an M.F.A. from the University of California-Irvine and a B.A. in Japanese from the University of Arizona. Her novel *Black Blood* was sold to W. W. Norton in 1996. She is now working on her memoir, *Discipline,* and researching her Choctaw, Southern Cheyenne background in Oklahoma.

Some years ago, there was all this fuss about the Harmonic Convergence. Around that time, I was in the Cambridge Public Library, and these middle-aged guys, who had pompadours, were putting up a display about Elvis. I had been idly thinking about writing a poem about Elvis, and I asked them which biography I should read. They recommended the Priscilla Presley book and damned another, which I found to be very helpful in the end, because it was nasty and disrespectful. I also rented some Elvis films and spent two days reading and trying to get into character. The night I finished the poem, I had a dream that Elvis's mother made him hug me. Anyway, that's how my poem came to be. I must say I was surprised when Papa made his appearance. Sometimes poems go off on their own like the juvenile delinquents they are, and the poet stands before the judge, whining I don't know what I did to cause this. Of course, this time, I was happy with what I had done.

Richard Blessing's books are *A Closed Book* (University of Washington Press, 1981), *A Passing Season* (Little, Brown, 1982), *Poems and Stories* (Dragon Gate, 1983), and *Winter Constellations* (Ashanta, 1977).

Don Bogen is the author of two books of poetry, both from Wesleyan University Press: *The Known World* (1997) and *After the Splendid Display* (1986). He teaches at the University of Cincinnati.

> The earliest drafts of "All Shook Up" date from the late '70s. I had seen a tape of one of Elvis's first TV appearances and was struck by the contrast between his personal presence—still vibrant after more than twenty years— and the '50s blandness of everything around him. It was as if the entire numbing context of the show—the clothes, the backdrop, the smiling host, even the Sunday viewing hour—kept announcing, "It's okay, he's safe," while the performance made it clear he was not. Working on "All Shook Up," I wanted a form that could carry both song and a certain bite. A variation on ballad seemed appropriate. The poem is one of several in *After the Splendid Display* that find origins in musical events. Mozart, Schubert, Stravinsky, and Bob Marley, among others, have their places alongside the King.

Neal Bowers's books include *Words for the Taking: The Hunt for a Plagiarist* (W. W. Norton, 1997) and *Night Vision* (BkMk Press, 1992). He is a Distinguished Professor in Liberal Arts and Sciences at Iowa State University.

> "On the Elvis Mailing List" is an attempt to show how completely Elvis is woven into our popular culture and how he permeates our private lives. The moment described in the poem is (to my embarrassment) factual; and I recall, all these years later, how eager my wife and I were to place our order for an album that seemed to capture not only the moody moment but also part of who we once were. "Conversions" deals more directly with the myth of Elvis, particularly with the ongoing sightings of a man who died almost

a quarter-century ago. Risen like the Jesus of rock and roll, he wanders the bleary zone of after-hours, waiting to reveal everything to the lonesome, faithful ones.

Van K. Brock founded Anhinga Press in the early '70s. His most recent poetry book is *Unspeakable Strangers: Descents into a Dark Self* (Anhinga, 1995). Brock is editor-in-chief of the first eleven volumes of *International Quarterly.* Current projects include an autobiography, a book of essays, and *The Scalding Eros: New and Selected Poems.* His essay "Images of Elvis, the South, and America" appears in *Elvis: Images and Fancies.*

After Elvis's death, I became interested in the intricate intertwining of Elvis as a myth, the media phenomenon and the cultures in America and abroad that, with his music and performance genius, created the myth. "Mary's Dream" is adapted from an account told to me by Mary, a woman from

New York whom I met at Graceland a year after Elvis's death, and "Sphinx" arises out of study and experience of Elvis, his life, and America.

Charles Bukowski is one of America's best-known contemporary writers of poetry and prose. He was born in 1920, in Andernach, Germany, to an American soldier father and a German mother. At the age of three, he was brought to the United States, raised in Los Angeles, his home for fifty years. Bukowski published his first short story in 1944, and began writing poetry, later, at the age of thirty-five. He died in San Pedro, California, on March 9, 1994, at the age of seventy-three, shortly after completing his last novel, *Pulp* (Black Sparrow Press, 1994). During his lifetime, he published more than forty-five books of poetry and prose, now published in translation in over a dozen languages. *What Matters Most Is How Well You Walk through the Fire* (Black Sparrow Press, 1999) is a recently released posthumous volume of Bukowski's work.

Lucille Clifton, Distinguished Professor of Humanities at St. Mary's College, Maryland, was named the recipient of the Lifetime Achievement Award for Excellence in Poetry by the Lannan Foundation. Recently, she published her thirty-first book, *The Terrible Stories*, with Boa Editions, Ltd.

Sam Cornish has published poems in the *Kenyon Review, Grand Street, Ploughshares,* and other periodicals. His poetry books include *Folks Like Me* (1993) and *Cross a Parted Sea* (1996), both from Zoland Books in Cambridge, Massachusetts. He teaches Literature and Minority Studies at Emerson College in Boston.

Maudelle Driskell's poem, "Talismans," appears in *The Made Thing: An Anthology of Contemporary Southern Poetry* (University of Arkansas Press, 1999), edited by Leon Stokesbury. Driskell works at Golden Key National Honor Society in Atlanta.

Cornelius Eady's books include *Victims of the Latest Dance Craze* (winner of the 1985 Lamont Prize), *Kartunes* (Warthog, 1980), *Boom Boom Boom* (State Street Press, 1988), and *The Gathering of My Name* (Carnegie Mellon Press, 1991), which was published by Carnegie Mellon Press and was nominated for the Pulitzer Prize.

Alice Fulton's books of poems include *Sensual Math* (W. W. Norton, 1995), *Powers Of Congress* (Godine, 1990), *Palladium* (University of Illinois Press, 1986), and *Dance Script with Electric Ballerina* (University of Illinois Press, 1996). A collection of essays, *Feeling as a Foreign Language: The Good Strangeness of Poetry,* was published by Graywolf Press in 1999.

My poems in this anthology are from *Sensual Math,* a book with several Elvis sightings. "Elvis from the Waist Up" is part of a sequence called "My Last TV Campaign." The sequence features an advertising executive of indeterminate gender who is trying to devise a campaign to sell the ancient concept of thou-art-that: a notion that dissolves boundaries between self and other. This persona learns of an orchid that evolved to resemble a bee, and the flower becomes a creative catalyst for the campaign-in-progress. In "Elvis from the Waist Up," the ad exec persona is looking at new homes. The conglomerate architecture of today's MacMansions inspire reflections on authenticity, imitation, and grotesque composites. A hayfever attack suggests the self/other boundary at the biological level, and an accidental visit to the Country Club implies exclusion/inclusion in the social realm. Toward the end, the speaker's thoughts are tinged with Elvis: the Elvis whose constructed upper body—greased, shaved, shielded by guitar—was deemed safe enough to air on TV while his dangerously "natural" lower half was censored. Delicious as it is to fetishize and excerpt, "Elvis from the Waist Up" gains when understood within the larger context of "My Last TV Campaign."

"Mail" is taken from "Give," a long sequence that reimages the myth of Daphne and Apollo. In Ovid's *Metamorphoses,* Apollo and Cupid are boastful rivals. Vengeful Cupid shoots two arrows: one pierces Apollo and makes him lust after Daphne; the other strikes Daphne and causes her to despise Apollo. In *The Metamorphoses,* people undergo grotesquely literal transformations. In my recasting, Apollo becomes a composite of Sinatra and dog, while Cupid is a blend of Elvis, flesh-eating botanical, and bee-like insect. Rather than shooting arrows at Apollo and Daphne, Cupid/Elvis mails them his hit records. They listen and fall into their respective postures of lust and loathing. "A New Release," also excerpted from "Give," is set in Daphne's mind after she has been turned into a tree. She is remembering the moment when she received Cupid's/Elvis's hit record and was infiltrated by its sticky notes.

I watched some Elvis videos as preparation for the poems. The early Elvis I found spellbinding. I could hardly take my eyes off him. The later Elvis, well—I watched him and felt—was it revulsion? Embarrassment? I could hardly stand to look at him. I sensed the complicity of embarrassment: the spectator's compassion, yes, but also the fear of infection, contamination, guilt by association. Dickinson wrote, "I like a look of agony because I know it's true." Embarrassment, a miniature agony, suggests that authenticity is not for the squeamish. I had this in mind when I wrote "About Face," with its tropes of reversal: cover and nakedness, the genuine and artificial.

"Some Cool" was perhaps the last piece I composed for *Sensual Math.* I wanted it to be short, but an early one-page version proved too easy. Rather than scrap the poem, I decided to open it up and create a longer, polyvocal structure. As a vegetarian and wannabe vegan, I was concerned about the suffering inflicted on animals. Yet I had never allowed or followed that commitment into poetry. It is hard to address injustice without resorting to polemics or sanctimoniousness, and I was aware of this as I wrote. At some point, the King crept into the thing. Two Kings, actually. I began the poem around Christmas when carols were in the air, including some sung by Elvis. The poem riffs on the rift between King and King. More importantly, it considers the distance between decorative, giftshop images of animals and actual animals. Here Elvis seems to figure for self-delusion, escapism, temptation, sentimentality, nostalgia, and American plenty. Ultimately, though, he's a bit player. "Some Cool" is concerned with suffering and the denial of feeling. I was writing about inconvenient knowledge, the truths we repress or deny in order to live comfortably, coolly, in this culture—a culture that creates and embraces all things Elvis.

Brian Gilmore is an attorney and a writer and poet from Washington, D.C. He is the author of *Elvis Presley is Alive and Well and Living in Harlem* (Third World Press, Chicago, 1993) and the forthcoming *Jungle Nights and Soda Fountain Rags: Poem for Duke Ellington* (Karibou Books, 1999).

Thom Gunn was born in England in 1929 and moved to California in 1954. He lives in San Francisco and has recently retired from teaching English at the University of California-Berkeley. Gunn's *Collected Poems* (Farrar, Straus, Giroux) was published in 1994. *Boss Cupid* (Farrar, Straus, Giroux, 2000) is his most recent book of poems.

> I really have little to say about these old, rather shabby poems. I don't even like them very much. The first of them did give me a limited notoriety since when it was published, people didn't write poetry about such a subject. It was a first, then, but a feeble first. It celebrates the emergence, in those great gutsy early songs, which were always to be his best. The pre-army Elvis.

Andrew Hudgins is a Distinguished Research Professor and Professor of English at the University of Cincinnati. His most recent books are *Babylon in a Jar* (Houghton Mifflin, 1998) and *The Glass Anvil* (University of Michigan, 1997).

> I wrote this poem after reading an article—perhaps even in *Penthouse;* I'm not sure—by a woman bragging about her "affair" with Elvis, if you can dignify it with that word. The whole encounter was pathetic that her pride in telling the story said something about American celebrity and the way that people react to it and define themselves in terms of it. Isn't this how characters in myth and folklore service the gods? At the same time there was a certain perverse energy in the woman's voice, her pride, and her anger at her ex-husband—as if a passionate Leda had overmastered Zeus without either one of them noticing she had done it.

Jon Hughes, journalist and writer, is a self-taught photojournalist and documentary photographer who began taking pictures in 1985, at the age of forty. Hughes has been on assignment around the world (most recently in Thailand and China), though he considers Cincinnati his major ongoing documentary project. Besides regular publications (in *Cincinnati CityBeat*, for example) and recent exhibits in the city (at the Taft Museum in 1997, and the Visual History Gallery in Hyde Park and the University of Cincinnati Tangeman Fine Arts Gallery in 1998), Hughes's work has been exhibited internationally, at the Phototeca de Cuba, and published in national publications ranging from the *Los Angeles Times* to literary magazines. Hughes's photographs have worked with poetry before—and perhaps even more closely—in his book, with poet Jeffrey Hillard, *Pieces of Fernald: Poems and Images of a Place* (Cincinnati Writers' Project, 1998).

Elvis is more than an international personality. More than a singer. Even more than a cultural icon. He is part of my singular memory, part of my youth, part of a place in my time. I was eleven years old in 1956 when Elvis first came to visit me, first by his sound on radio, then by his image in magazines and on TV, and finally by the word, his name, in print. Elvis. A one-word name. Elvis. Like a famous South American soccer player. His sound, his image, and his name remain a part of my time and my life. So, it did not take much persuasion for me to join Will Clemens in a road trip to Memphis, the place that so influenced this great American artist. To the land of blues and country and Sun Records.

The photographs in this collection were taken in Memphis and Cincinnati over an eleven-month period between November 1999 and October 2000. It is a very subjective look, my impressions, of how Elvis is represented and remembered by many people, in many ways, for many reasons. His name is now part of our lexicon. His image, unfortunately, has lost a sense of reality. But his music, really the most important legacy, should not be forgotten, because it was his voice, his sound, his energy, that preceded everything else.

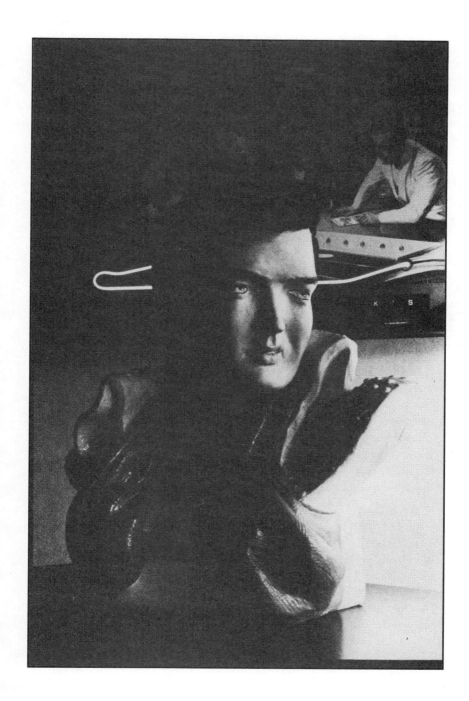

Fleda Brown Jackson's most recent collection of poems is *The Devil's Child* (Carnegie-Mellon University Press, 1999). She teaches at the University of Delaware.

When I was fifteen—in Arkansas, which is next door to Mississippi—I was kissing the Elvis poster on my wall. I would also kiss the Ricky Nelson poster, evidence, no doubt, of a deep split in my psyche. Over the years, I have favored first the one, then the other—but mostly the dark, brooding King, who arrived at the junction of musical history and changed it forever, who arrived at the junction of my adolescence and changed me forever. I am writing a book of Elvis poems because I will always be bound to him, my adolescent heart both attracted and revulsed. He keeps showing up, wanting attention. To write these poems, I read his biographies; I tracked his post-mortem appearances; I made him up when he left no traces.

Some of the poems are biographical, some are more about Elvis face-to-face with a world that has left him behind. I figured—for example, in "Elvis Reads 'The Wild Swans at Coole'"—that if he were hanging out at McDonald's in Kalamazoo, why wouldn't he come to Oxford, Mississippi, too, for the First International Elvis Conference, to defend himself, if not out of sheer curiosity? Or maybe they paid his way as the distinguished guest speaker, fresh blood in the musty halls of academe, chosen to bridge the gap between the spirit and the intellect. But as in all my poems, here, his heart's the rebel. He tries to do what they want, being a nice Southern boy, but the effort sucks the blood right out of him, leaves him weightless, flying off the end of the poem, back to the drum beat of the human heart. I really didn't want either side to win. I kept the King within fairly regular triplets in this poem, even when he thinks he's off on his own.

"Elvis at the End of History" started out as an essay submitted to a contest (which I didn't win)—Describe Your Elvis Sighting in 250 Words—in a Lansing, Michigan, newspaper. I was at our summer cottage in Michigan at the time. I figured that the Elvis I would encounter there would be as old as our cottage, as our outhouse—gentle, vulnerable at last. I found that he had softened into my own song. This, I guess, is where I join the split parts of my psyche, not able to tell whether I'm hearing my own singing or his. When the I, or the feminine voice in the poem, visits the "Twenty-four Hour Coin-op Church of Elvis" in Portland, she begins to believe she really is Elvis, and this is a good thing. This poem stays formally loose, swings its arms. She is returning, or longing to return, to the organic, approximating pure feeling, untainted by irony, which is probably where the true Elvis lives.

Herbert Woodward Martin's most recent collection is *Galileo's Suns*, published in a double volume titled *Dunbar: Suns and Dominions* (Bottom Dog Press, 1999). Martin won the 1998 Mellen Poetry Prize for a single volume of poetry.

In my poem ("Miss Rosie Mae . . ."), I am trying to catch the spirit of a real Miss Rosie Mae, who was a bit perturbed if not outraged at the overactive hormones the young girls loosed in that theater. I think we may safely say that Presley made us overtly aware of our sexual nature with his more than provocative wiggles. I think that Miss Rosie Mae approved of sex or, say, a good joke, for that matter, with the best of us, but I think it was always a private matter for her. She was raised in an era of a bit more decorum and a lot less screaming. Still, I suspect she was familiar with all the young girls who screamed for Frank Sinatra, and she may have been one of them.

I think what I most wanted to accomplish in this poem was the sense of atmosphere created by the young audience at the "Ed Sullivan Show" on those Sundays when Presley appeared. Sudden and unexplainable waves of emotion overwhelmed the audience wherever they were watching. And I wanted to catch as much as I could of Miss Rosie Mae's larger-than-life character, speech-rhythms, and tone. I wanted this to be as good a photograph/recording as possible, so readers might associate this Rosie Mae with their own.

Lynne McMahon's newest collection of poems, *The House of Entertaining Science,* has just been released from David R. Godine. She teaches at the University of Missouri-Columbia.

Joyce Carol Oates's most recent collection of poems is *The Time Traveler* (Lord John Press, 1987). Her short stories have appeared in the 1963, 1964, 1965, 1967, 1969, and 1970 editions of *Best American Short Stories*. She teaches in the Creative Writing Program at Princeton University.

"Waiting on Elvis, 1956" is really about the loss of youth and innocence—the old days of rock and roll, gone forever.

David Ray's poetry books include *Sam's Book* (Wesleyan University Press, 1987), *Wool Highways* (Helicon Nine Editions, 1992) (which won the 1994 William Carlos Williams Prize from the Poetry Society of America), and *Kangaroo Paws: Poems Written in Australia* (Thomas Jefferson University Press, 1995). His latest book, *Demons in the Diner* (Ashland Poetry Press, 1999), won the 1999 Richard Snyder Memorial Prize from the Ashland Poetry Press (Ashland, Ohio). He lives in Tucson, Arizona.

David Rivard's most recent book is *Bewitched Playground* (Graywolf, 2000). He teaches at Tufts University.

Nearly twenty years after having written this poem, I can see that "the part of the soul that doubts, again and again" is a whole lot less important than it liked to think. Besides, it's the mind that does the doubting, not the soul (the mistaken insight being a clear symptom of the way my mind was trying to distract attention from itself back in those days).

The real drama is not between desire and doubt, but between compassion and judgement. You stand on a windy headland overlooking a beach, pastures and orchards stretching out behind you, and shoot an arrow into the ocean, and the ocean forgives. This is a fact. Hard to say whether knowledge of it would have helped Elvis.

He was an American, however; and that has certain advantages in this life. I believe these advantages are described quite nicely by Greil Marcus, when he refers, in *Invisible Republic,* to that place he calls "the old weird America":

> . . . where the ruling question of public life has to do with how people plumb their souls and then present their discoveries, their true selves, to others.
>
> God reigns here, but his rule can be refused. His gaze cannot be escaped; his hand, maybe. You can bet: you can stake a probably real exile on a probably imaginary homecoming. . . . It's limbo, but it's not bad; on the fourth day of July you get to holler.

James Seay's most recent collection of poetry is *Open Field, Understory: New and Selected Poems* (Louisiana State University Press, 1997). He teaches at the University of North Carolina at Chapel Hill.

In my poem "Audubon Drive, Memphis," I'm not thinking so much about the music of rock and roll as about the way rock stars get hurled into systems of gratification they rarely know how to negotiate with, short of excess. But more than that I'm thinking about how we get so vicariously intimate with them—at any rate, their addresses, diets, and designers of choice—and other public figures whose candlepower we choose as part of the illumination of our own hopes. It's an old story, of course, only now it's fiberoptic and laser-beamed, and tomorrow it may be virtual-reality computer-driven. In some instances we remember where we were when they died. We're that close. In the case of Elvis, I wasn't, despite what the poem implies, "parked outside a gas station / just over the bridge from Pawley's Island / with the radio on." That's just the way I scripted it, knowing what I know of Elvis's life. The cars and all, I mean. Actually, I was on Pawley's Island, in a convenience store, buying some orange juice for breakfast, and I saw the newspaper headline THE KING IS DEAD. When JFK and Martin Luther King were killed, I was where I say I was in the poem. I wept both times, but that doesn't keep them out of the overlap with Elvis, for whom I was sorry but not moved to tears. So there they are together, at least in the economy I've imagined, still waiting for the pool to fill. And we know more or less everything that is happening to them.

Dan Sicoli has published over 250 poems in numerous small press and literary magazines throughout the United States, Canada, and Germany. His poetry has been anthologized in *A New Geography of Poets* (University of Arkansas Press, 1992), *La Bella Figura* (malafemmina press), *Sweet Nothings: An Anthology of Rock and Roll in American Poetry* (Indiana University Press, 1994), and *Italian-American and Italian-Canadian Poets: Volume II*, a bilingual anthology edited by Ferdinando Alfonsi of Fordham University. His audio poetics work can be found on several poetry audio cassette anthologies, including *Sanctuary 9* and *American Contemporary Headcheese.* A life-long resident of the working-class neighborhoods of Niagra Falls, New York, Sicoli has worked as a baker, district sales manager, letter carrier, housing coordinator, printer, cheese packer, and rhythm guitarist. He is co-founder and co-editor of *Slipstream* Magazine and Press.

Elvis was the first rock 'n' roll pop star to be marketed successfully in a big way. His influence continues to be felt today, although I suspect it has more to do with the image he projected than with his music. This is not to say Elvis didn't produce some respectable and lasting work, some of which still sounds fresh and vital. Listen to "Mystery Train" or "That's All Right (Mama)."

My poem, "All Shook Up," comments as much on fashion and sincerity as it does on rock 'n' roll. It was Buffalo, in a nearly condemned dive with high leaky ceilings and decaying walls, where the seed for this poem grew. Punk had just broken and was now the in thing. On stage a band of three young, lanky short-haired guys in T-shirts played punk versions of well-known pop songs, often taking liberties with the original lyrics. When they covered Elvis, the lead singer sang, "I'm on drugs . . . I'm all fucked up!"—instead of "I'm in love . . . I'm all shook up!" for an audience of fashionably punk suburbanites.

.

Terry Stokes has published several books, most out of print, but he is currently working on more "politically incorrect" poems for a New and Selected collection.

About "The Elvis Elevator": Some of it's true; some of it's false. Yes, along with the rest of the eighth-grade class at Colebrook Consolidated School, I was a member of the Elvis fan club. Yes, I have visited Graceland, and the details regarding the Hare Krishnas hawking books are true, and the recycling the roses is true, as is the garish shopping mall across the way from the entrance to Graceland. I found the shopping mall to be garish American tacky, like some of the outfits Elvis wore in Vegas; therefore, I loved it.

There is an Elvis elevator in downtown Cincinnati; and I give guided tours to it.

It was also striking to me that on Vern and Gladys's headstones, there was such a disproportionate amount of information. For me, this is where the true women's liberation movement began. So it seems we can thank Elvis for that, too.

Dabney Stuart's recent books include *The Way to Cobbs Creek* (stories) (University of Missouri Press, 1997) and *Settlers* (poems) (Louisiana State University Press, 1999). He lives in Lexington, Virginia.

Celebrity strikes me as one of the most abject of poverties, and Elvis as one of the most pathetic celebrities. It seems fitting that he continues to be a central icon of popular culture. He was manipulated and, finally, grotesquely isolated. My poem seeks to embody something of this condition—Elvis Presley's incongruity and sadness, his bewilderment.

Elizabeth Ash Vélez is currently editing an anthology of poetry— *Surviving Love: Literary Therapy for the Brokenhearted.* She teaches writing and Women's Studies at Georgetown University.

I have loved Elvis since my best friend, La Brenda LuQuire, introduced me to him in Birmingham, Alabama, in the early fifties. My father declared him a "dope fiend," banned his music from our home (I played "All Shook Up" a hundred times a day), and by the time I was twelve (in 1957), I was ready for the sixties.

In 1993, I was reading *Madame Bovary*, and I came across the following passage: "The two black sweeps of her hair, pulled down from a fine center part that followed the curve of her skull, were so sleek that each seemed to be one piece." I thought of Elvis's fine hair, thought of France and Tennessee, thought of how Colonel Parker ruined Elvis, how poor Emma was ruined by Monsieur Lheureux. . . .

Diane Wakoski is the author of more than twenty collections of poetry, including her recent series, *The Archeology of Movies and Books* (Black Sparrow Press, 1999), which includes four volumes to date, one of which, *Jason the Sailor* (Black Sparrow Press, 1993), is the source for her poem "Blue Suede Shoes."

In my poem, I want to use the trope of shoes as the denoter of a person's psychological and social condition in the twentieth century. The legendary blue suede shoes that Elvis wore when he sang the Carl Perkins song became a parallel image of Cinderella's mythic glass slipper, the tiny magical shoe that represents a girl's natural aristocracy, and it's American counterpart, the mythic ruby slippers created by Hollywood for Judy Garland as Dorothy in the screen version of *The Wizard of Oz*. They symbolize her ability to walk away from the confusing place the tornado set her down, back to her beloved Kansas.

In the original story, Dorothy's magic slippers are silver, my totemic color, the color of the moon, thus giving me a reason to identify with her. But Hollywood, in order to show off their new Technicolor technique, decided the slippers should be red. This film has become a part of American myth about the importance of home, the virtues of honesty and the omnipresence of illusion in our culture. I loved coalescing the blue suede shoes, the ruby slippers (originally silver), and the transparent or white Cinderella shoe (indicating purity) in my poem. For me, the excitement of the poem was to reveal the trope of these shoes as an emblem of American culture as they are, of course, Red, White, and Blue.

David Wojahn is the author of five collections of poetry, most recently *The Falling Hour* (University of Pittsburgh Press, 1997). He directs the Program in Creative Writing at Indiana University and also teaches in the M.F.A. Writing Program at Vermont College. [Note: A collection of his essays is due out in 2001, from the University of Arkansas Press.]

The six poems included here are excerpted from *Mystery Train,* a sequence of thirty-five poems which are about late twentieth-century American history and culture, seen through the lens of rock and roll music. Many other figures of course appear in the sequence, but Elvis obviously occupies a special place in it. Most of the poems devoted to Elvis were written in the late 1980s, and derive from incidents related in Albert Goldman's grimly cynical study of its subject, which at the time was the only full-scale Elvis biography. But some of the incidents described are more autobiographical, based on a number of visits I made to Graceland over the years. And one poem, the description of William Carlos Williams's impressions of Elvis, is a wholly imaginary monologue. Nearly all the poems of *Mystery Train* are sonnets or near-sonnets, even the W.C.W. poem, which conceals a couplet sonnet in the lineation employed in many of Williams's later poems. "Pharoah's Palace" is the exception to the sonnet rule; it's a loose sestina. When writing the *Mystery Train* poems, I wanted a hoary traditional form to collide with contemporary subject matter, and I immensely enjoyed planning such a marriage. (Not everyone who reviewed the book liked this mix, however: one particularly bone-headed reviewer went on and on about a couplet in the sequence that rhymed "etc." with "ooo-wah"). One more aspect of the poems is worth mentioning: they were all written during a period in which I was living in Spain; instead of composing odes to bull-fights and the Alhambra, I found myself writing about rock and roll; in retrospect, this seems like the wisest decision I could have made.